Lessons from The Cotswolds

Two Old Fogies Dodge Disasters while Walking Through the Cotswolds

LELE BEUTEL

Lele Beutel loves to meet and chat with fans!

Reach out to her at apedersen6@comcast.net.

Cover and book design by Publishing Hackers

Paperback ISBN: 979-8-9902359-9-1

Ebook ISBN: 979-8-9985227-0-3

Table of Contents

Also by Lele Beutel...

The Camino Connection: Connecting with Life and Commemorating a Death While Walking on the Camino de Santiago

What God Wants You to Know: A Daily Devotional

God Answers: A Daily Devotional

Lele's Selah: Prayerful Poems that Inspire Hope

The Reignbreaker: A Young Adult fantasy

Flora's Story, A young girl and her family survive the Nazi and Russian regimes of 1940s Germany

1

For those who may be old

but still want to experience the exuberance

of a life well-lived!

On our way to the Cotswolds

   And to my husband Mike, whose accompanying support through a crazy 30-year adventure is humongously appreciated!

From two old fogies...

To the seniors who aspire to travel, but sometimes doubt their ability to do what they've always dreamed of, we offer this token of how we accomplished a dream trip and survived to tell the story!

"Travel advice: Always keep your sense of humor with you. There will always be that bump in the road, and you certainly don't want it turning into a mountain. Laugh about things, don't take life so seriously. "—Donna Ayers

The quotes used at the beginning of each chapter were submitted by members of my Facebook groups:

- Senior Travelers on the Camino

- Senior Travelers and Trekkers

A heartfelt thank-you to each and every one of you!

The United Kingdom

The Cotswolds

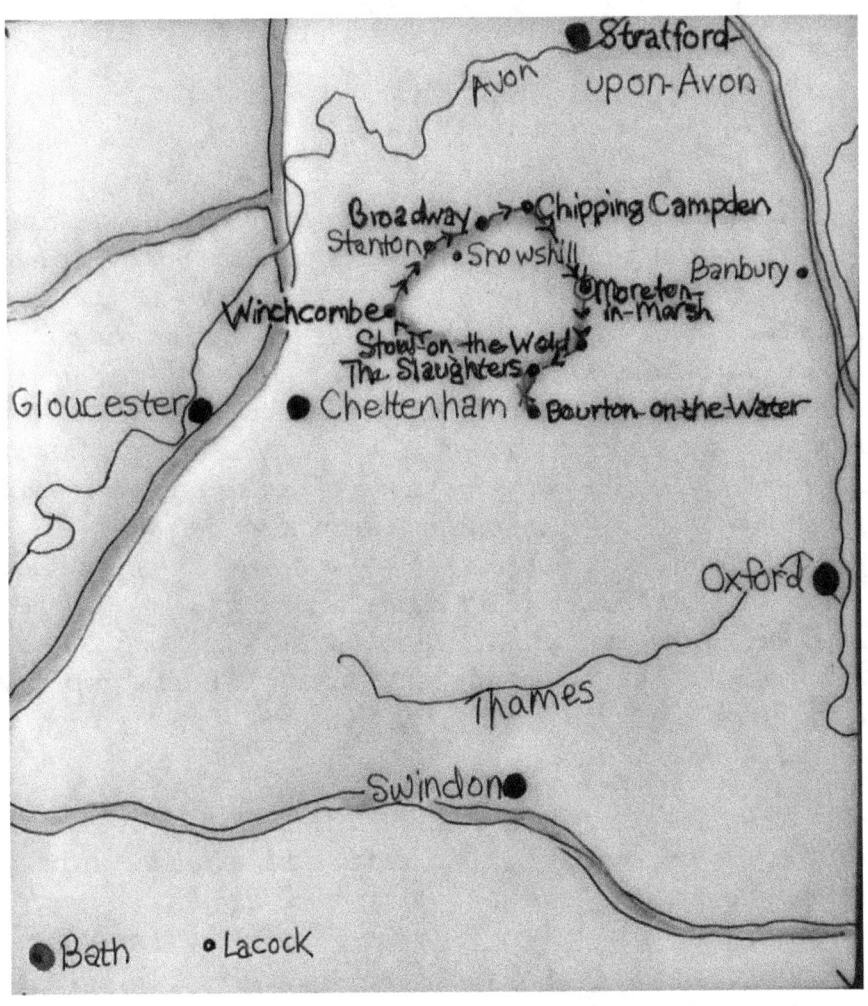

Introduction

O h, dear Lord! Help!" I exclaimed as I tried to pull my foot out of the sucking, two-feet-deep muck that had grabbed and held onto my shoe. I tried to keep my balance without falling into the waiting muddy rut in front of me as I thrust my other foot forward, holding it in the air for one uncontrollable moment. No other choice. I tried to pull my foot with the shoe intact out of the guzzling sludge. It was hopeless. "Dang!" I said to myself as I pulled my foot out of the shoe to free it. Waving my arms around for balance as I held my socked foot up in the air, I reached down to pull my shoe out of the mire. I felt like an acrobat in a circus who showed up to perform a spectacular feat only to discover she had to do it on one leg! As I freed my shoe from the mud's grip, my equilibrium gave way, and I fell front-first into the waiting brown pools of water.

"For the love of God!" I shrieked. And, just then, I glanced back to see my husband, Mike, circling his extended arms in the air and trying to grab at anything while standing on one leg sunk feet-deep in the ooze. With the other leg wavering in the air, he teetered back and forth like a bobble-headed juggler trying to balance on a ball while holding an umbrella in his teeth. And I wondered, at that moment, what in the world we

were doing on this sloshy, sludgy, rut-ridden trail between two
fences in the middle of the Cotswolds!

After experiencing the exhilaration of walking on the
Camino de Santiago, a 500-mile pilgrimage through Spain, in
May 2023, I came home exhausted but excited. The two weeks
walking from St. Jean Pied de Port, France, to Logrõno, Spain,
then from Sarria to Santiago de Compostela, Spain, covering
125 miles of the pilgrimage, had completely changed my
perspective on life. Not only did that special time open my eyes
to a world where people walked in unity of purpose toward a
shared goal, but it delivered me from lingering regrets after the
death of my son. Meeting so many openly kind people along
the way, from every part of the world, and making friends
where language barriers were nonexistent, had completely
changed my heart. I was so inspired by my journey that I ended
up writing a book called *The Camino Connection.*

On my way home from this pilgrimage, I couldn't wait to
tell Mike about what I'd encountered. And I just knew he'd
want to do something similar with me. He couldn't go this time
because walking so many miles was prohibitive for him. He'd
had two leg surgeries to correct the varicose veins that resulted
from spending 30 years on his feet as a lab technician, and he
knew his limitations. But, as I flew from Vigo to Madrid, after
an exuberant entry into Santiago, Spain—the grand finale of
the Camino where pilgrims lay down any remaining life
burdens carried along the way at the feet of St. James in the
cathedral dedicated to him—I racked my brain about how I
could do another walk with Mike. I really wanted him to
experience at least some of what I had.

At home, I explained to him how different a trek, or walking tour, was from a car, bus, train, plane, or boat excursion, where the traveler sees limited views—most of them from a window.

"I saw and met the Spanish people," I enthused. "I watched as they fed their cattle and corralled their sheep. I heard roosters crowing in the morning, and I saw farm dogs who looked me straight in the eye. I trekked beside cows on their way to fields and barns, and I looked out over vine-covered stone walls to hills decorated with colorful flowers. And I breathed in forests of fragrant eucalyptus trees. It was breath-taking, even life-changing!" How could I explain the beauty of it?

He stared blankly at me. "Sounds great!" And I knew he'd never understand unless he experienced something like it.

After showing him my pictures and telling him numerous stories of the multi-lingual people I'd encountered, I began my search for another journey, this time a less strenuous one that we both could enjoy. But where to begin? Where could I find a walkable area where we could complete a week-long trek? It would be too daunting to commit to more than that the first time. We'd need to see how it went. I tried to narrow my search to what would be doable at our ages and stages of life, Mike at 81, with limited walking capability, and me at 71, with diminished energy capacity.

Many parts of Great Britain appealed to me. I loved the thought of hiking through the Lake District where so many famous authors and poets once lived. Or over the trails that run throughout Cornwall, the famed land portrayed in the BBC series, *Doc Martin* and *Poldark.* What about the Yorkshire towns where Author James Herriott lived and described his animal adventures as a vet in the 1930s, 40s, and 50s in *All*

Creatures Great and Small? Or the beautiful Welsh coast, where the legendary King Arthur lived? Would the captivating Isle of Skye hold our attention for a week? There were so many places I'd never been!

I'd seen all of Rick Steves' travel episodes on television. My husband often jokes about how many times I can watch the same episode! I never get tired of seeing places I've never been but hope to see one day and ones I've experienced. "I remember that town!" I'd yell out when a familiar scene popped up on the screen. One place always caught my undivided attention. It was one we'd never visited: the Cotswolds. I was drawn to its picturesque and historic landscapes and, of course, the accents of the people. Watching Steves traipse through wooded areas and scenic, sheep-filled pastures, separated by charming wooden fences with openings called "kissing gates," I thought, "Who wouldn't want to go there?"

I started reviewing trips coordinated by Mac's Adventures, the outfit I'd used to make my arrangements for walking on the Camino. And I noticed that they had a "slow walking series" with one called "Cotswolds in Comfort."

"Sounds great!" I thought. "Right up our alley!" The distances between towns were between six and nine miles. And I thought, "That's doable." We could go three miles in the morning, rest at a pub, maybe partake of some ale, then continue on in the afternoon. This would be more leisurely and possible to accomplish in a day, unlike the Camino, where I walked between nine and 19 miles every day. I knew we'd have to work up to this though. Mike could easily do two miles a day. We did that much while walking our two dogs. But six to nine miles was a stretch. We'd have to set a goal of walking more miles each week to prepare.

The accommodations chosen by Mac's looked wonderfully quaint and historically rustic with a charming local flavor.

"Perfect!" I thought. I showed the pictures on their site to Mike and checked the costs. Reasonable. It was the best thing I'd seen. We talked about this trip as an option for May 2024. It was October 2023. By November, we were signed up to go. And in January 2024, I had my airline tickets, and we were set to go. We just needed to start walking more!

I trekked between three and five miles each day. To prepare for the Camino, I'd covered between six or seven a day, so, I thought, a little less would be sufficient preparation for this journey. Mike didn't get in as many miles, but he tried to walk at least two or three miles each day.

"What do you think?" I ventured one day in March, as we walked the dogs over the last quarter-mile around a lake toward home. It was a 50-degree day, brisk but sunny—just the way I liked it. "Will you be able to walk six to nine miles when we get there?"

"We'll just have to see," Mike wasn't too reassuring.

"Hmmm," I sighed with no idea what challenges lay ahead for us. "Are you sure you want to do this?"

"Yes," he nodded. "Let's do it!"

"Ok." I'd learned to accept what I could get. Never any guarantees or promises. He seemed alright now. That was good. We'd just need to step into this adventure a bit blindsided. All we could do was try, right? But would we be able to walk the distance once we got there? No one knew. I just had to trust that it would all work out.

And, as we set our sights on our own unique pilgrimage, with the main goal being that we could mutually experience something life-changing and meaningful, we wondered what unforeseen challenges we'd encounter and if we'd be prepared to face them. I prayed then that God would fill in the gaps!

A bit about the Cotswolds

I knew very little about the Cotswolds before we left. My impression was that this was a scenic and quaint area of England, filled with rustic, honey-colored limestone buildings. The views I'd seen on the travel shows captivated me, because the area exuded just the kind of olden-day, romantic ambiance I loved to breathe in. If you live in the United States, like me, it's rare to see anything ancient, except in a museum, and it's difficult to find anything that dates before the 1800s, especially in the Midwest, where I live. You might find historic towns that've been preserved or restored for tourists. Some have a certain allure because of the famous people who once lived there or because of their reputation as a river-town or sight-seeing destination. I think of places like Hannibal, Missouri, home of Mark Twain; Galena, Illinois, where Ulysses S. Grant once lived; Abilene, Kansas, with its cowboy and gunfighting history and home of Dwight D. Eisenhower; and Springfield, Illinois, where Abraham Lincoln resided. Where I live, near Kansas City, we talk about Jesse James coming through or how the wagon trains stopped here before leaving for the Oregon Trail. These are our great points of interest. But they all date back to no earlier than the 1800s. In contrast, one Cotswolds town boasts an inn built in 975 AD!

For some geography, the Cotswolds, in southwest England, are bounded to the west by Gloucester and Cheltenham, to the north by Stratford-upon-Avon, to the east by Blenheim Palace and Oxford, and to the south by Bath and and Swindon.

"The area is characterized by attractive small towns and villages built of the underlying Cotswold stone (a yellow oolitic limestone, rich in fossils), many with magnificent 'wool' churches that grew out of the prosperous medieval wool trade. It is these villages...beautifully preserved, that more than anything have come to be associated with a Cotswold identity," says *cotswoldjourneys.com.*

Many weavers moved to the Cotswolds, because wool was the foundation of the economy from the time the Romans brought sheep to England and used the fleece to make uniforms for their army. The most successful period was 1250-1350 AD, when wealth from the wool trade led to the construction of churches, manor houses, and other buildings. The name Cotswolds comes from the words "cots," which means sheep enclosure, and "wolds," which refers to the area's hills. Some say the name comes from "Cod's-wold" or "Cod's high open land," "Cod" being an Old English name.

Rick Steves, in his episode on "West England," says, "As with many fairy-tale regions in Europe, the present-day beauty of the Cotswolds is a result of an economic disaster. Wool was a huge industry in medieval England and Cotswold sheep grew the very best. According to a 12th-century saying, 'In Europe, the best wool is English. And in England, the best wool is Cotswold.' It's a story of boom and bust and then boom again. Because of its wool, the region prospered. Wealthy merchants built fine homes of the honey-colored local limestone. Thankful to God for the wealth their sheep brought, they built oversized churches nicknamed 'wool cathedrals.' But, with the rise of cotton in the industrial revolution, the region's wool industry collapsed. The fine Cotwold towns fell into a sleepy depressed time warp, becoming sleeping beauties. Because of that, the region has a rustic charm. And that's the basis of the new prosperity. Its residents are catering to lots of tourists. And the Cotswolds have become a popular escape for Londoners.... Everything you see was made of the same finely-worked Cotswold stone, the only stone allowed today. Roofs still use the traditional stone shingles....

"For centuries...people came from as far away as Italy to buy the prized Cotswold wool fleeces. You can imagine with 20,000 sheep sold on a single day, it was a thriving scene."

The disintegration of the wool industry brought about an economic stagnation that lasted for centuries. It wasn't until the last hundred years that it became a popular destination for visitors, property buyers, and retirees. With the rise of automobiles, the area became more accessible. When the tourists came, they found a group of quaint and picturesque villages little changed over the years. And this led to their overall appeal.

These descriptions, plus the fact that the Cotswold boundaries extend about 40 miles across and 120 miles from top to bottom, made me think, "We can manage this trip! Even at our age and condition!" It seemed like the perfect place to start a manageable journey. Between the historic and local appeal, the fact that they spoke English (and I do love their accent!), and the smaller distances between towns, we agreed that this would make for an ideal trek for two old fogies.

Our hearts elated by all the possibilities latent in this new adventure, little did we know what really lay in store for us....

Lesson One

Prepare realistically!

Preparing to walk with our dogs

B*eing realistic means being well-informed. Researching for an adventure is the best way to prepare for any adverse encounters or situations. 'What if' is a very valid question. In other words, try not to have expectations. Expectations may frustrate you when they are not what happens. Have PREFERENCES then prepare for anything."—* Joy Paguirigan-Kayaban

Planning for any adventure that includes other people involves sitting down and agreeing on what you'd like to accomplish together. I've learned the hard way that, if you don't adequately discuss how you're going to handle eventualities, or at least the ones that are most likely to happen, you'll invariably you'll invariably find yourself setting out on an obstacle course that ends up being more like an unmanageable maze. For you and the other person or persons. I experienced this during another trip with a colleague.

One of my biggest mistakes was agreeing to walk with a lady I barely knew and then trekking together over a many miles through unfamiliar territory. We'd never done shorter excursions together to see if our walking styles meshed, and I had some hesitations when she first asked me if I would "do the Camino" with her. I didn't know her very well, but I'd wanted to experience this pilgrimage for many years, especially after my son died, and I thought it would be a healing venture for me. So, I agreed to do it with her.

To prepare, we talked about walking together on weekends, but interruptions and obligations got in the way. We did a two-mile trek twice that included one short uphill climb. I did notice a lot of huffing and puffing on the hill, and, seeing this red flag, I asked, "Do you think we're ready for this trek?" My thoughts raced ahead to the 15-mile climb over mountains, which was part of the itinerary. Her answer was an emphatic "Yes!" So, I left it at that.

On the trip, we attacked the first-day uphill climb, and I was shocked to see how unprepared she was. I'd spent months walking up to seven miles a day. Sadly, she had not. As we ascended the steep paths, I moved ahead just to get enough momentum to be able to make the climb. Then I waited for her to catch up. Five miles into the trek, and about five hours in, we stopped at the only restaurant along the trail. She cried as we ate because her hips and knees caused her so much pain. I encouraged her to continue and slowed my pace so she could keep up. It took us nine more hours to reach the next town, which was about 10 miles away. Others had managed the whole climb and descent in six. We walked alone through sleet and fog; all the other hikers had passed us long ago.

Every day, she wanted to take a taxi at least halfway to accomplish the nine to 19 miles we had to cover. Since I'd assumed, when we talked about the trip, that taking taxis was a non-starter for us, after a week of cabbing, I told her I wanted to try to walk the whole distance each day. We could meet up at the end of the day at the places we'd booked. That worked well for me, but she was dismayed that she couldn't do the same. I felt bad for her and encouraged her by saying this was her first try and, with a better understanding of what it required, she could try again and, next time, walk more miles. I felt afterward like the trip was a success for me. I'd accomplished what I set out to do: walk at least 125 miles of the 500-mile pilgrimage. But, for her, it was a complete disappointment, and she would not talk about it or share memories when we returned. That made me sad, since she was the only person who'd experienced the same lovely scenery and met many of the same amazing people as I had. But she just didn't want to relive any part of it because of the pain it caused her.

In retrospect, I should have been more astute to her physical condition, and she should have been more honest about her limitations. She did admit before we left that she was getting steroid shots in her knees. That should have been another red flag. I discovered as we walked on the Camino that she was also suffering from severe hip pain. If I'd known her situation better and understood the intensity of some of the up and downhill hikes we'd encounter, I would have insisted on postponing the journey until we were both more prepared. Or, I would have gone alone.

After the trip, my regret was that we hadn't set clearer expectations of what a successful journey looked like to each of us. It would have been helpful if we'd had an agreement beforehand, like: "If either of us can't walk the distance, let's agree that it's ok if that person takes a cab, but it's also ok if the other person continues to walk alone, as long as it's not a medical emergency where one of us needs the other person to be present. We can meet up later at a designated location." This would have avoided any bitter feelings at the end of the day. Also, having an understanding ahead of time that we didn't have to walk together the whole way, allowing for a difference in pace, would have been helpful and freeing. We could be there to help the other person when needed, but we didn't have to be "tied at the hip," expecting the other to always walk beside us.

Looking back, I knew I was meant to walk on the Camino. It was something God had put on my heart many years earlier, and the experience was life-changing and healing for me. Should I have done it with her? Only God knows. But her insistence on going was what got me there, and for that I am very thankful.

I've learned over the years from this and other experiences that it's always a good idea to "check things out with God" first. If you feel uncomfortable or anxious about tackling an adventure, there may be a reason. Listen to your heart. Pay attention to His nudgings. There may be something you're not aware of going on. If you feel at peace with a plan, it's probably ok to move ahead with it. Recently, I was reminded of this when I read a quote by Joyce Meyer in her book, *The Confident Woman Devotional*, where she says, "It is good to have plans, and I believe we should plan boldly and aggressively, but we must be wise enough to know that our plans will ultimately fail without God." Hmmm. Pretty insightful advice. In other words, don't forget to include Him in your plans.

Of course, being married, Mike and I had to set our own mutual expectations. We'd traveled extensively together over the past 25 years, but we'd never attempted a "walking tour." And, since he's 10 years older than me, and has more physical limitations, I understood that I'd have to "bend a bit" if I wanted to walk with him. Since the purpose of the trip was that he be able to experience at least a taste of what I did on the Camino, I was all right with that. And, because I'd had to slow down, and take cabs, for a week during the previous trip, I knew I could do it, and be patient, which was a stretch for me since my personality is Type A and Mike's is not. I've had to learn how to negotiate and compromise on many occasions with him, not always happily, but willingly, with God's help!

This time, I made sure we talked about things. We decided to practice walking together several times a week, so we both knew what to expect. Usually, we walk alone with our two dogs, Andey and Barney. Mike likes to take Andey the Corgi, and I take Barney the Shweenie (a Shi Tzu/Dachshund mix). The reason we often go separately is because the dogs like to compete with each other and see who can get ahead. They pull mercilessly on the leashes and drag us along. We have been unable to train them not to do this, so we suffer through their yanking down the sidewalks. It's just way easier to walk apart! Even when we start out together, I usually go ahead, since Barney and I enjoy going faster, and Andey, though the same age as Barney, is content to go at a slower pace with Mike. Sometimes people ask why we don't walk together. I'm sure it looks strange to them. I then explain how and why we walk at a different pace.

But now, we'd walk at least partway together with the competing dogs so we could see how we'd need to adjust when we were trekking without them. Since I was able to see how he performed with his leg issues, and understood his ability, it was easier for me to "settle into" a sort of mindset of patience and slow down my quicker steps.

We also made sure to bring waterproof shoes and raincoats, because we knew that rain was in the forecast for the week we'd be in England. And we wanted to walk, even if it rained—another thing we'd agreed on ahead of time.

If you've ever planned and proceeded with a trip, you know that there are countless things that can go wrong. And you're tempted to complain about them. The worst culprits are the food, the accommodations, access to technology, the waitstaff, rude people, the weather, the clothing you didn't bring, having what you need when you need it, the timing of transportation, not understanding the signage or language, and physical issues. We agreed to limit the complaints, because we knew there'd be plenty of opportunities to be disappointed if we chose that route. And I know that the more you express negativity, the worse things can feel.

Together we determined another objective for the trip. Besides experiencing a "behind the scenes" trek through this part of England, we wanted to meet the people. I consider myself "God's secret agent," as I explained to my granddaughter who asked me once why I always try to converse with people who cross my path.

"I'm always seeking opportunities to encourage them in their faith walk," I explained.

Mike is a good conversationalist, and he also likes to get to know people and share his experiences with them. We both love to meet people when we travel, and we're always surprised by how many people from other countries we end up befriending wherever we go. We were both looking forward to seeing what doors God would open for us on this journey. Who knew what He had in mind?

The idea of walking through the Cotswolds grew larger and more real each day as we approached our departure date. Since we'd be in England anyway, flying in and out of Heathrow Airport, I thought we might as well spend some time in London and Oxford. I'd been to London twice before, but there was one place I'd always wanted to explore but never had the chance: the Churchill War Rooms. We could also book a bus tour to Windsor Castle, Stonehenge, and Bath—three places on my bucket list. I'd always wanted to visit Oxford and the colleges there. Especially since I knew they were attended by people like C.S. Lewis, T.E. Lawrence, and J.R.R. Tolkien. So, I padded the front end of the trip with two days in London and the back end with two days in Oxford, which was on the train route between London and Moreton-in-Marsh, where we'd start and end our eight-day Cotswold trek.

As you'll see, regardless of how well you anticipate what you might encounter, and you plan accordingly, you will always end up being confronted by unexpected and unplanned events along the way. Things you could never anticipate. We'd determined to start each day by praying that God would take care of us, have us where we were needed, and be in every eventuality. That would explain why we *were* able to survive so many surprises along the way. And each new circumstance reaffirmed to us things we knew but had to experience again so they would sink in. This was, I believe, the real reason we went through them!

Whatever you do, there will always be unforeseen things you just have to take in stride if you want to thrive despite life's ups and downs. How *will* you handle them? This is the million-dollar question! As I look back on how we overcame obstacles and dodged disasters, I find it hopeful, heartening, and sometimes hilarious!

Lesson Two

New friends are everywhere!

To the War Rooms

"Friends are where you try to be one."—Anne Williams

Our first-met friends showed up in the Chicago O'Hare Airport on the way to London. At Wolfgang Puck's Express in the terminal, I turned to Federico and Sandra, who were sitting at a table next to us, and I asked them to take our picture. From South America, they were on their way to Rome, the Amalfi Coast, Florence, and another coastal

Italian town. Yes, many of the dreamed-about, bucket-list places in Italy. After snapping our photo, they were eager to talk. They asked where we were going. And as we sipped glasses of red wine, I shared about my trip on the Camino and how it led to this trip to the Cotswolds.

"I want my husband to experience a taste of what I did while walking on a trail among other like-minded hikers," I explained.

Federico's response was far from what I expected. With tears in his eyes, he told me about how he'd heard about the Camino 10 years ago from a good friend at work, who encouraged him to go, elaborating her own adventures and the meaning she'd gleaned from the pilgrimage. When she passed away unexpectedly, he vowed that one day he would do the trek in her honor. Then he asked what I'd loved most about it.

"From the very start, you feel a connection with the other people walking, who all say 'buen camino' as they pass by," I responded. "You're all there for a reason. Often, it's for physical or mental healing, or to get through a life transition."

His eyes followed my words. And, I could tell, his heart did too.

"It wasn't like anything I'd ever done," I emphasized.

I thought how it was the reason Mike and I were here now, getting ready to pursue another trail-blazing adventure with the hope that he could experience at least part of what I had on the Camino trail.

As I told them about my life-changing Camino experience, I noticed that Sandra was rubbing her leg and knee. I asked her what had happened. She said she'd hurt her leg when she fell getting on a train as they transferred back and forth to the airport on a quick trip to Chicago during an hours-long layover. She could barely walk now because of the excruciating pain, and they were getting ready to board a flight for their weeks-long adventure. She was apprehensive as to how much walking she could do now. I asked her if she believed in God. She said she did. My next question: *Could we pray for her leg and knee?*

"Yes," she said without hesitation.

So, Mike and I got up, stood behind her, put our hands on her shoulders, and took turns praying out loud for her. We asked God to heal her, so she'd be pain-free and able to walk as needed. Since we had to leave for our flight before they did, we never got to see if her leg and knee were better. But, knowing how God works, I believe they were.

We arrived in London's Heathrow Airport early Sunday morning. It was May 19th and a beautiful day. We quickly got a taxi with a friendly cabby, who pointed out some of the sights on the way to our hotel near Paddington Train Station. After checking in, resting briefly, and changing clothes, we hailed another cab to the Churchill War Rooms. The driver could not pull up in front of the museum, since some streets were blocked off, so he dropped us off as close as he could at an entrance to St. James Park. This ended up being a blessing in disguise. We'd never seen this section of London, and, as we wandered around the park, we were captivated by the lush, landscaped green spaces and abundant wildlife, including herons, swans, geese, pelicans, a shooting fountain, and a quaint medieval-looking building near a pond.

I thought about another Sunday morning on our first trip to London in the summer of 2005. We were staying in a bed-and-breakfast near Hyde Park and wanted to go to a church we'd read about that was near Buckingham Palace. Westminster Chapel is an evangelical church famous for being the church where R.T. Kendall preached between 1977 and 2002. I'd read Kendall's book called *Total Forgiveness*, and I'd heard him speak on several television shows. His way of reaching people with a message of forgiveness through a belief in Jesus Christ had touched me so profoundly that I wanted to see the church that was his base for many years. So, we were up early on a Sunday morning and ready to trek across Hyde Park to get to a 10 o'clock service in time. On the way through the park, I remember being overwhelmed by the quiet serenity, as we walked beside magnificent trees that lined the walkway. I was also awed by a parade of uniformed soldiers with plumed hats that rode by on horses on their way to Buckingham Palace. It didn't take us very long to get to the church; we arrived by 9 am, and we walked up the steps to the arched front door. It was locked. As we descended to the side of the church, we spied a door into an alleyway, and, suddenly, a woman, carrying a tray of pastries, stepped up. Heading for the door, she unlocked it and said, "Come this way!"

We followed her through the alley-door and were immediately greeted by another woman standing in front of a door that opened onto a bricked courtyard behind the church.

"Come in! Come in!" the second woman exclaimed and pointed inside the door. "We've been expecting you!"

Surprised, but not shocked, since we'd come to expect the unusual and unexpected on this trip, we entered a room and sat toward the back in chairs near the door. We weren't sure what this was all about, but we found out we'd joined a pre-service prayer meeting. We chatted with an American man next to us who was in London on business for an international doughnut company. At the front of the room, a man and woman started the meeting once the room was full. They began with a prayer, then they asked if others wanted to pray.

It was one week after the July 7th subway bombings—a series of suicide attacks that targeted commuters on London's public transport during the morning rush hour—and I was curious how these participants would respond. I listened as, one at a time, voices sprang up from around the room in different accents, and I realized that the people praying were from all over the world. Some were from Africa, Asia, parts of Europe, the States, and many from London, plus who knows how many other areas. The united voices were praying for peace and protection in London and around the world. And many "amens" rose up around the room in response to the prayers.

"Amen!" I whispered in agreement, and I shuddered at the spiritual power I felt emerging from this group of about 50 people, all crammed in this small room. "Unbelievable!"

At the end of this powerful prayer session, we all funneled through the door and made our way into the church. Mike and I sat in a pew toward the back. When the service started, a band played on a stage in front, and a minister prayed and preached after others shared about ministries they supported around the world. During a hand-shaking, introductory time, before the sermon, we met a young couple sitting in front of us who were missionaries to China. We told them we were thankful for their efforts, and they beamed. After the service, we went with others into a reception area for coffee, and we met a few others, including an Asian woman who walked with us to her favorite restaurant nearby, where she suggested we have lunch. Sadly, she didn't join us, but we appreciated her kindness. The whole experience was a bit surreal for us—having just arrived in London and being thrust immediately into a gathering of international, like-minded people, who loved to pray as we did. I will never forget this memorable experience and, since then, I've wondered if we'd encounter anything like it again.

Now, here we were in London, with a very short timeframe to see and do as much as we could. At the War Rooms, I was enthralled as I made my way through narrow halls, past small rooms set to represent the way they looked during the war, and through an expansive Churchill memorial. As I walked back in time, I experienced historical reminders of the events that occurred and the people who navigated them within London's interior as Nazis leveled their gun-sites on London in 1940 and 1941. I'd always been fascinated by Winston Churchill's life, and this impressive, well-organized museum captured the essence of how he led the nation to victory during WWII. What captured my imagination most was how, after so many defeats, he withstood the political onslaughts and stood his ground, even as he suffered great rejection from political "allies." Because of his persistence, England endured through the war.

After visiting the War Rooms, we strolled to Buckingham Palace—a short distance away. We were awestruck again by the majestic Queen Victoria Memorial, which we viewed from every angle. Finding jet lag catching up to us, and our legs saying, "That's enough!" we spotted a cab conveniently parked beside the palace. Of course, it was meant for us! And we were thankful for it. We hadn't even considered walking across London to get back to our hotel!

After a short rest, it was time for dinner, and we had set our sights on an Italian restaurant named Bella Italia next to the hotel. It looked inviting, and it was just too convenient. I thought, "If we drink a little too much wine, we can easily get back to our rooms!" So, we walked over and checked out the menu. Everything sounded so good! And there was a table for two waiting for us in the small, covered patio area in front of the restaurant. It reminded me of the outdoor seating areas in the places we'd visited in Italy and France. Perfect! It was such a pleasant evening, we couldn't resist.

Our tiny table was wedged between two larger, crowded tables. After squeezing into our seats and gazing at the menus, we were thrilled when we were handed glasses of excellent Sangiovese wine. Within minutes of sitting down, a couple at a table next to us turned around and started to converse. We were surprised by their open friendliness. Vasenti and Shashti were originally from India, had lived in Kenya and Abu Dhabi, and now lived in London. Vasenti works as a mechanical engineer, and Shashti is a pharmacist. At the table with them were a sister and brother-in-law. We had a meaningful conversation about the places they'd lived, and they asked us where we were from and where we were going. I told them the story of my walking on the Camino (my usual opener, since it was the reason we were here) and how inspired I was by it and how it led to our walk through the Cotswolds. We talked for a while, but then their food arrived—two delicious-looking pizzas. We'd ordered the beef and wine ravioli. I think we were all happy with what we'd chosen.

We scarfed down our pasta dishes, drank up every drop of the wine, and excused ourselves. The time change was hitting both of us, and, after little sleep on the plane, we were exhausted. Our goal was to stay up all day, which we did. But now, at 6:30 pm, we had to hit the hay before the hay hit us!

"Such kind people!" I thought as we said good-bye. "I hope we see them again." We didn't, but I wish we had. And that I'd thought to get their contact information.

The next day, we were up by 5 am, which is not unusual for us! At home, we're up around 4:30 to spend time doing devotions, reading, feeding and walking the dogs, exercising, etc. But we also go to bed early. We went to the lobby at 6:50 am to catch a cab at 7 bound for Victoria Coach Station. Our cabby was a young Indian man who made sure we knew where to enter the station and where to go to grab a bite to eat inside. We were thankful for his attempt to help us find our way.

It was difficult locating the right terminal for Premier Tours, but we finally found it on the other side of the street in another building. We found our group and, after chatting with a nice older couple from the States who confirmed that we were in the right place, we heard them call out the number for our tour to Windsor Castle, Stonehenge, and Bath, with dinner in a pub. On the bus, and in our seats, we were greeted by Toby, our tall, dark and curly-haired, young guide. And we were on our way. Though I'm not a big fan of bus tours, especially after my hike through Spain, I was thankful to be able to see what we did on this trip. Thankful, except for….

As Toby walked up and down the bus aisle greeting people on either side and discussing the sights, his face suddenly changed, and he took on a seriously ominous expression.

"Just one thing I want to make sure you know." His smile warped into an evil grin. "If you're late getting back to the bus on *any* of our stops, we won't hesitate to LEAVE WITHOUT YOU!"

I cringed.

I reflected on another trip where Mike and I *were* left behind by our group. We'd signed up for a train trip through Switzerland in 2014, and we looked forward to traveling through the countryside viewing gorgeous, snow-peaked mountains, spectacular waterfalls, and villages filled with Swiss chalets nestled in valleys. The thought of this took my breath away! Well, on our way back from Jungfrau to Interlaken by train, our group made a lunch stop at the Kleine Scheidegg Train Station, where they'd set up tables for us to enjoy a three-course lunch. Mike and I finished the last course quickly and made our way to the public restrooms before heading back to the train. I told our guide, who stood by an exit door, that I was going downstairs to use the facilities and to *please* wait for me before leaving.

When I descended the stairs to the one-room ladies' facility, I was confronted with a long line of women. So, I waited, and waited, until it was my turn. By the time I got back upstairs, the lady-guide was gone, along with our entire group. I met Mike exiting another station door at the same time, and we both hunted for the bright-colored teepee that stood beside the track and our waiting train. The guide had made sure we spotted this marker before we came inside to dine. Just as we identified it, and ran toward our waiting train, filled with our fellow-travelers leaning out of the windows, it began to move! We both stood there, stunned, as we watched our train head down the tracks! And we wondered what to do. Just then, I saw a uniformed conductor standing between the tracks and I ran up to him. Thank God he spoke English!

"Our train just left!" I said breathlessly as my mind whirred with memories of sayings I'd heard about the reliability of Swiss trains. Apparently, they were true...to our detriment!

"Get on this one!" he said quickly. "It will take you to the same place!" He ushered us to some steps onto another train. It was completely full, except for two seats, so we slid in beside a German couple who sat across from each other in the narrow, wooden seats and refused to make eye contact with us the whole way, staring blankly out the windows. Mike and I, eyes wide, faced each other. How awkward! They made it very clear we weren't welcome to sit there, but we had no choice.

As the train zipped over the tracks toward Interlaken, we realized that we had no idea where to get off. How would we know when we arrived at our destination and where to go to rejoin our group? Thankfully, a group of Americans sat behind us. Hearing them talk, I turned and asked if they knew where we should get off to meet our bus. One of them knew the right stop. When we screeched to a halt at one station, she yelled, "This is it!" and we hopped off. As we exited the train, we saw our group across the tracks, boarding a bus. And we ran to join them.

Once on the bus, as the guide walked up and down the aisle counting heads, I told her they'd left us behind and how we'd taken another train. She was shocked. Apparently, another couple, not with our group, had gotten into the car and she had counted them with the others, thinking she had everyone. Though that was a very anxious time for us, we saw how God intervened with the right people at the right time and brought us back safely. Though I was somewhat irritated that the guide did not wait for us, I was thankful that He'd made sure we got there.

On this bus-tour of England, as I reminisced about being left behind once before, I shuddered.

Our first stop was Windsor Castle, and I was surprised to see that it wasn't just a castle set off by itself in the middle of nowhere, as I'd imagined. The historical buildings of the Windsor estate were surrounded by streets full of shops and cafés. We parked in a large parking lot for buses and walked up a circuitous street, around many corners, then uphill to a road that led to the castle. I remember seeing a train engine on display called "The Queen," streams of flags hanging overhead, and a shop with dog paraphernalia. After passing a quaint stone chapel with an arched wooden door, we followed a crowd, single file up a sidewalk to the gated entry of the castle grounds. At the top of a hill, Toby handed us tickets and pointed in the direction of the street we'd just climbed. "Meet me at the bus at 11:15. And, *remember*, if you're late, WE LEAVE WITHOUT YOU!" It was 10 am.

After meandering up a road that wound past several interesting octagonal-shaped brick turrets and walls with arched windows and doors, we passed by many outbuildings on the way to the castle. But we didn't stop, because *we knew* we only had one hour to see the main parts of the castle, and we DIDN'T want to be late! We finally found the main entrance to the castle and wandered through many large rooms filled with family paintings and antiques. We took in as much as we could as fast as we could. It all seems like a blur now, and we weren't allowed to take pictures, so I have only a few faint memories of what was in those rooms.

Finally, making our way toward the exit, and longing for some caffeine, we found a café down some steps, but they weren't serving coffee, so we quickly left the building and discovered a coffee and pastry vendor outside on the road. Holding cups of steaming hot coffee, we gazed around at a beautiful fenced green area that lay pristinely between the buildings, surrounded by a road. We made our way through the grounds toward the gate-exit, but I desperately wanted to see St. George's Chapel before we left. I knew this would be my only chance to see it. Mike didn't think we had time. It was 11 o'clock. But I ignored his pleas and ran as fast as I could into the church, dashing past a woman stationed at the door who looked at me crossly, made my way up the aisle to peek into the interior, where so many royals were buried, including Queen Elizabeth and Henry VIII. Then I zoomed outside to find Mike waiting. We high-tailed it toward the exit.

Once outside the tall iron gates, we looked around for the way back to the coach parking lot. We saw no sign of the streets we'd walked through to get to the castle. Absolutely nothing looked familiar. No sign of a dog shop or banners or an engine.

"Shoot!" I wanted to say something else, but I didn't. "Which way is it?"

"I have no idea." Mike was as oblivious as I was. We looked around then approached a man sitting on a low wall by the sidewalk.

"Any idea where the buses are parked?" I asked. "Is this the street to the parking lot?" I pointed to a nearby road. He had no idea but thought we needed to take the next street down. So, we walked toward it. It didn't look right, so we kept going. We walked. And walked. Still no sign of the familiar streets. We realized we were totally lost. And it was 11:10. We ran as fast as our cramping legs would carry us and came to a river park. I saw a man who looked like he was a local, sitting on a bench, and I ran up to him.

"We're lost!" I puffed. "We're trying to get to our bus, but we can't find the parking lot!"

To this day, I am thankful for this "angel." The kind man immediately stood up and pointed up the street.

"Just there, around that corner," he smiled calmly. "You'll see it past those shops."

"Thank you! *Thank you!*" I panted, sweating profusely. We ran as fast as we could (which, for us, is a slow trot) up the street and through an alley between some shops. On the other side was the Coach Parking Lot. *And there was our bus!* I ran up to Toby, who stood in front of the bus, looking grimly toward us and pointing to his watch. It was 11:20.

"You're *late!*" He grimaced and stabbed me with his finger. I was ready for a warlock curse of some kind to be pronounced over us.

"I know!" I huffed. " *We got lost!*"

"Well, we'll have to take this time off *the next stop*, you know!" He frowned, staring down at me as Mike came up.

33

Without another word, we climbed onto the bus and slunk past all the other bus-trippers, who proudly sat in place, having arrived in time. Many gave us stern side-glances as we tiptoed stealthily past them. Head down, I could see them out of the corner of my eye, since I couldn't look any of them in the face. I never felt so ashamed. I took my seat and tried to make my own excuses. *"We did get lost!"* I thought. *"Give us a break!"* Mike climbed in beside me, and we both stared out the window as the bus pulled out of the parking lot.

Our next stop was Stonehenge. I'd seen many pictures of the huge stone monoliths, but I didn't know exactly what to expect. I'd read that it took over 1,000 years to build this historical monument, that the stones weigh up to 30 tons each, that no one knows how it was built, and that some of the stones originated in Wales. And I wondered how close to the stones we could get. We drove a ways to get to a parking lot, where we could take a shuttle or walk to the site. Since the trek was a bit long, we took the shuttle. Again, we had an hour. I looked at my watch.

"We can't be late this time!" I muttered. Mike nodded and we hustled as fast as we could from the drop-off to the circular path surrounding the stones, which were roped off. A large open field with a circle of monoliths stood stalwartly in the center. On the other side of the path, an inviting grassy expanse full of birds, flowers, and butterflies was just as captivating, I thought. But it was fenced off from the public. Black birds with white faces sat on the fence posts cawing and gazing defiantly at all the passersby as if to say, "Just try to get past us to pick a flower! *Just try it!*"

I heard someone behind us say, "They're not *nearly* as large as I thought they'd be!" Mike whispered to me, "Yeah, well you try to haul them all the way from Wales!" I laughed. We thought they were pretty darn impressive and definitely worth seeing. Plus, it was a perfect 70-degree day to enjoy a romp around the beautiful English countryside.

I'm happy to say we made it back to the bus in plenty of time *this time.* In fact, we were early! Even after dashing through the visitor's center and using the facilities, we boarded the bus ahead of everyone else. And, as each person appeared at the top of the bus steps, some later than others, we looked up from our seats and smiled smarmily as if to say, "Yea, well, some of us *do* actually know how to be on time after all! *Haha!*"

And then there was Bath. Named after its Roman-built baths, the town is designated as a UNESCO World Heritage Site. Founded in the 1st century AD by the Romans, who used its natural hot springs as a thermal spa, it also became an important center for the wool industry in the Middle Ages. In the 18th century, under the reigns of George I, II and III, it developed into an elegant spa city and reflected the ambitions of John Wood Senior (1704-1754), Ralph Allen (1693-1764) and Richard "Beau" Nash (1674-1761), who made Bath "into one of the most beautiful cities in Europe, with architecture and landscape combined harmoniously for the enjoyment of the spa town's cure takers," according to *Unesco.* Famous for its Roman history, Georgian architecture, thermal-spring spas, and museums, it became widely known, especially during Jane Austen's era, as a place for wealthy Londoners to bring their marriage-eligible children to find good suitors.

Museumofbathstone.org says: "Around 160 million years ago, the land...was under a warm, shallow, tropical sea. Tiny fragments in this warm sea became coated with thin layers of calcium carbonate, forming egg-shaped stones known as 'ooliths.' Over time they became compressed to form oolitic limestone—the stone that built Bath." This type of stone is found throughout the Cotswolds.

Being hyper-vigilant about having only one hour to see the city center, we zoomed past Bath Abbey, the Roman Baths, the Thermae Bath Spa, the Temple of Sulis Minerva, and the Pump Room (a famous historic restaurant), taking pictures and glancing through windows and doors. Thankfully, I'd seen these places in Rick Steves' episode on Bath. Sadly, we didn't have time to partake of any of them or venture inside. "Maybe a reason to return," I thought. But we did linger long enough to enjoy watching a man surrounded by a flock of pigeons hold out his arms and hat to them as passers-by came over to admire his burgeoning bird fan club. Some held out their own arms as the man encouraged the pigeons to climb all over them while others took pictures. *Not me!*

We wandered into the square in front of Bath Abbey, a Gothic-style church built from Cotswold stone with a tall, perpendicular front, castle-like columns and embrasures on either side of an arch, and rows of arched stained-glass windows. I'm sure the inside is spectacular! I thought. Two men with long hair, one wearing a felt hat, long coat, and leather boots, the other with hair pulled back, a muscle shirt, and shoeless socks, greeted us with lively music. One played the accordion, the other a guitar, and they serenaded us as we passed by. I appreciated their efforts and wanted to tip them, but time was of the essence.

Glancing at our watches, we raced down the narrow street that led to our pickup point and realized we still had five minutes to spare. So, we stopped for some gelato at a shop on the way. It was there that I discovered that all the coins I'd been saving from our 2005 visit to London were worthless! The girl at the shop handed them back and said that the newer coinage looked different, and these were no longer honored. Dang! So much for holding onto foreign cash for almost 20 years! Oh well! Back in my bag they went.

Standing on an island where three streets converged, we licked our lemon-ice gelato cones and peered over at a lush park where families gathered around a gazebo on chairs and blankets to enjoy the amazing weather, still in the 70s and clear. Soon, the bus came barreling up, and we were the first to climb aboard, *again.* As others ascended the steps, we grinned proudly.

We drove past streets full of limestone buildings on our way out of town. Most impressive was the Royal Crescent, a row of 30 terraced houses considered to be the best examples of Georgian architecture in the UK. We whizzed by, and I snapped a picture of Jane Austen's hangout among them.

Our last stop was Lacock, a tiny town in the Cotswolds, where we'd dine at a local pub called George Inn, established in 1361. Sitting at a small, antique wooden table, devouring fish and chips, I gazed around at the dark-wood fixtures, beamed ceilings, and old stone fireplace. I noticed that two ladies we'd met at the castle, Wendy and Darlene from New Hampshire and Massachusetts, sat nearby. We talked and compared our food choices and talked about the pub and the tour. Again, more new friends!

Lacock wasn't among the towns we'd trek through later, so we were glad we had this chance to see another quaint example of Cotswold history. After eating, we walked around, admiring the architecture. Because of its allure, parts of the Harry Potter series were filmed here. We passed by rows of honey-stone homes with vine-covered walls and jutting bay windows that allowed for a peek into welcoming rooms. The surrounding stone walls were adorned with pretty orange poppies.

One restaurant sported limestone at the bottom of a half-timber-topped building. Bay windows with square-leaded glass panes stood out from the plaster, supported by upside-down, L-shaped wooden pieces attached to the wall. All the buildings had slate roofs. We appreciated the quaintness of it all, especially the arched wooden doors that welcomed visitors. Looking around, I felt like I'd traveled back to 18th century England.

"Wouldn't see this where we live!" I sighed.

Back at the hotel, after an hour-long, sleepy ride back to London through the countryside, we took the elevator up to the first floor. We'd noticed a bar area there and decided we needed a night cap. So, we sat at a table on an open deck and ordered our favorite wine. It was cool and pleasant, and we enjoyed talking about the day as we sipped our Sangiovese. At one point, we looked at each other. It was our last day in London. Tomorrow, we'd have to maneuver through Paddington Station and find the right train to Moreton-in-Marsh. We shuddered to think about some past experiences with European trains.

Our most stressful encounters with trains were in Italy, where the train stations are frenzied and chaotic, especially in the cities. On one adventure in Venice, I remember standing under flashing overhead signs that announced the arrival of trains, hoping we wouldn't miss ours when it came. When our number flashed on the screen, we quickly made your way to the platform, trying to find the right one before it took off again within minutes. We weren't sure which cars were first-class and which were economy, or if this was even the correct train. There were no signs or confirmations of any kind. So, we asked a conductor on the track. He shook his head and refused to help us. We weren't sure if he didn't speak English or just didn't like helping tourists! We approached people getting on the train and asked if this one went to Slovenia, and a kind soul confirmed we were ok. We breathed a sigh of relief.

On board, before the train started moving, we looked for luggage racks, usually by the exits, with space for our bags. If not, we had to stuff them in front of our seats or overhead, if they fit. On a trip from Florence to Perugia, the racks were all full, and we sat with our large luggage in front of us, cramped in our seats for hours. Off the train, we had to lug these monstrosities down many steps from our platform and up more steps to the terminal. That was the last time we brought huge suitcases on a trip! Now we only travel with carry-ons. Especially after the airlines misplaced our checked bags on the way to La Spezia one year. We had to wear travel clothes for three days as we trekked over goat paths in the rain between the towns in Cinque Terre while they located our luggage. What dumb tourists we were! I sighed now just thinking about these indescribable experiences.

As we sat reminiscing now over wine on a hotel rooftop, our hope was that the English trains weren't quite so challenging. Maybe more user-friendly? But we didn't know. We'd never attempted a train trip here before. On our previous trip to London, we'd taken cabs wherever we went, or the hop-on-hop-off bus. We looked at each other over our glasses of wine. So far, we'd appreciated the new friends we'd made and the places we'd seen the last two days. That made our travel time, which had been relatively easy except for being shamefully late from the castle, very special. But now, we wondered, "Could we manage the train tomorrow at our age? Could we move quickly and not miss our ride, like we had in Switzerland? Could we figure out how to get our tickets at the kiosks and read the signs and find the right track and train when it arrived? Could we board it in time?"

Mike winced at the thoughts, and I cringed.

Lesson Three

Expect the unexpected

The outdoor market at Moreton-in-Marsh

"Travel with an open mind, heart, and just let it unfold beautifully in the moment like it's your last. The sudden stops or fails can be unexpected delights."—Ann A. Moreto

The day started well with a typical English Breakfast of eggs, ham, sausage, black pudding, baked beans, a grilled tomato and mushroom, and buttered toast, with a cappuccino at Bella's next door. Now it was time for our dreaded trek to Paddington Station with luggage in tow. Even at 9 am, we had to push past clumps of people on the sidewalk as we made our way down London Street. Shops selling produce and clothing displayed their wares out front. So, we had to maneuver around browsing people without entering the street, where cars buzzed by. At the corner, only a block away, it was so crowded that we had to press our way forward, surrounded on every side, across a busy main street when the light turned, and the pedestrian "walk" sign popped up.

We entered the station along with the horde and found a kiosk close to the entrance. I walked up to it and scrutinized the buttons, trying to figure out what to press. I thought I'd figured it out and pushed a button, with the hope that I'd gotten the correct tickets, when a young woman came bounding up to us. Her hair colored bright red, with a nose piercing and tattoos, she cheerfully asked if we needed help.

" *We do!*" I nodded enthusiastically, trying to figure out why she'd approached us but happy to have help, regardless of where it came from or why. "I think I got the right tickets but now I'm not sure where to get on the platform!"

"Where are you going?" she asked matter-of-factly.

"To Moreton-in-Marsh."

She verified I'd gotten what we needed then walked us over to a large overhead sign and pointed up to identify the train number we wanted. After that she turned and showed us where to stand to get on the train.

41

"Thank you! You're a God-send!" I exclaimed before she turned to leave. I wanted to hug her!

"The universe always supplies what you need when you need it," she responded.

"I believe it's God," I said brightly.

"It's more about energy," she smiled.

"Yes!" I said. "He *is* energy and He's *light.*" She nodded. We could agree on that. I asked her why she came over. Why had she wanted to help us?

"You stood out to me," she said simply. "It was like you had this aura around you. You were shining. I couldn't help it! I knew I needed to help you."

And I thought of what we'd just been discussing: energy and light. I particularly thought about the power of God to draw people together. Did we, as His believers, give off some sort of light-energy or "aura" that people could see? I had always thought it was possible. But this confirmed it. And I thanked Him at that moment. Then I hugged and thanked her.

"She's an author," Mike said out of the blue, as we got ready to leave. I looked at her and asked if she'd heard about the Camino de Santiago. She hadn't, so I explained what it was and about my trip and the book I'd written about it.

"It's all about connections," I explained. "Kind of like what we're experiencing right now—connecting with people who turn up unexpectedly to help us!"

I showed her my book online, and I hoped she'd read it, since I relate so many ways God revealed Himself on my trek through Spain. She brought up her own website—

sinikkartristry—and told us she was an artist from Norway. I expressed interest in her information and artwork.

"Maybe we can connect online," I offered.

I was very grateful for her kindness at that moment when we needed guidance but didn't expect it. And I was reminded that you never know who will step up to offer a hand when you need it. Often, it's the people you least expected.

Thanks to Sinikka, we located and boarded our train by 9:52, and we were able to find good seats near the exit. I found space for my bag on a rack, but we had to keep Mike's between us at our seats. The train made many stops, but each one was called out clearly and in a timely manner. At 10:25 they called out "Moreton-in-Marsh," and we deboarded quickly. In the station, we met a couple from Virginia standing by the restrooms who were also traveling through the Cotswolds. Later, we saw them again in town. It's always good to come across people you've met when you're far away from home. For some reason, it makes me feel like I'm still within reach of the familiar.

Moreton was first mentioned as a Saxon settlement around 577 AD, says *AI Overview*. Following the Norman conquest of Britain, the township was part of the monastic property held by Westminster Abbey in London. Abbott Rickard of Barking began developing it as a medieval market town between 1222 and 1246. The name Moreton was first recorded in 1278 as *Meretun* and comes from Anglo-Saxon words meaning a settlement (tun) beside a lake (mere). Moreton-in-Marsh is close to a complex of lakes and a duck pond.

I looked at a map on a board by the station and on my phone for directions, but I couldn't accurately judge the distance to The White Hart Royal Hotel from the station.

"Let's try to walk," I suggested, since we didn't see any cabs around or numbers to call for one. We set out walking up an adjoining street that looked like it went toward town. Just then a man approached us, and I stopped him to ask, "Do you know how to get to High Street?"

"Yes!" he sounded promising. "Just turn right at the end of this street. Follow that street to the end and turn left. That's High Street!"

Yay! I was so relieved we hadn't opted for a taxi. We followed his directions, found High Street, then walked about two blocks past honey-stone-built shops and restaurants. Then we saw The White Hart Royal Hotel sitting right in front of us across a street! And it looked inviting.

Opened in the 1600s and originally called The White Hart, it was famous for hosting King Charles I on two occasions, according to their website. An important stop on the first turnpike road through Moreton-in-Marsh, it became known as a coaching inn when the owners, the Winslows, expanded its stable to house up to 70 horses. The railway brought more visitors after 1853, and new owner, Robert King, added to the inn and renamed it The White Hart Royal. It is now run by The Coaching Inn Group, who refurbished the hotel but kept its ambiance intact by respecting and retaining its historic Georgian features, including the Cotswold stone exterior.

It was too early to go to our room, so we left our luggage at the front desk and set out to find a good place to eat lunch. We've found, as we travel, that it's unusual for us to end up in the wrong place. In fact, we never have! For some reason, we seem to have a sense for what we're looking for and always find it! On High Street, we noticed many tents set up in an open-air market. We found out that Moreton-in-Marsh is known for its weekly Cotswold Market. And it's only on Tuesdays, the day we just happened to be here! Another God-wink. I'd grown used to these unique moments that were always completely unplanned for, when we'd just happen onto something that added a special touch or memory to our adventure. We decided to visit the market after we ate. Our stomachs were just too persistent—reminding us that we were starving!

We passed by more quaint limestone buildings and ran into a friendly man with a cute dog that could've been one of our dog's twin brother. Of course, we had to stop and talk to the man and pet his small dog, whose soft, white hair resembled Barney's. Mike can never resist conversing with other dog owners, and this was the first of many impromptu canine-related visits on our trip. Farther down the street, we discovered the Lynwood and Co. Café and a perfect, creamy-vegetable soup made with wild garlic and served with sourdough bread and cappuccinos. Delicious!

After eating, we wandered to a shop nearby called Alchemy, where I found some body lotion. Then we went across the street to check out the open-air market. With a wide assortment of produce, clothing, accessories, jewelry, THC products, etc., I found a ring and a sweater I liked. On every trip, I try to get one piece of jewelry, like a ring or earrings, to remind me of our adventure. This was no exception. The sweater would come in handy, since I realized how much the damp coldness seemed to seep into my bones. I'd packed some fleece tops. But that wasn't enough. Brrrr! I was shivering. At one tent, we saw the couple from Virginia from the train station, and we waved.

Back up the street, past the hotel, we found the Black Bear Inn, where we got a beer and a glass of Chardonnay. The tavern was busy, crowded, and popular. We enjoyed our drinks, but not as much as listening to the accents of the local people. It was close to 2 pm now, and we could check into the hotel. So, we traipsed back down to inn and proceeded to the front desk. Ana, the receptionist from Eastern Europe, ushered us outside through a lobby door and across a landscaped courtyard, where brick paths lined with greenery led to rooms on all sides of an open area full of tables topped with red umbrellas and surrounded by chairs. We followed her to our door, which had two tall, black vases topped with bushes on either side of it. The wall next to door was covered with lush wisteria that draped white flowers—like a 19th-century bouffant hairdo with long tendrils of hair hanging beside it. Ana used an old-fashioned key to open the lock, and, as we entered the room, we were flabbergasted by what we saw.

We decided that ours must be the nicest room at the hotel. How we ended up with it, only God knows. But I couldn't imagine there were any that were much nicer. The room was humongous. This was no doubt at least a four-star hotel, I decided. Maybe five star. As we crossed the expanse to plop our suitcases down on tables near the side-by-side twin beds, we heard classical music drifting toward us. And we noticed fluffy flowered pillows propped prettily against a beautifully upholstered headboard behind the beds. Thick, white comforters overlaid with tapestried coverlets beckoned to us to climb inside and experience their soft warmth. Sketches hung on the white-plastered walls, portraying an owl, a rabbit, a hedgehog, and a deer. They added to the charm. Above us, dark wooden beams swept across the ceiling. It all gave me the warm feeling of being in an Old English cottage.

On the other side of this bit of heaven, a large adjoining bath area boasted a porcelain tub on pedestals with a white towel draped over the side. A tray full of toiletry items, with a washcloth, a bathmat, and a rubber ducky, straddled the tub. I envisioned a beautiful, porcelain-skinned lady, dressed in medieval attire and a Victorian-style bonnet, holding her arm out toward the tub, inviting us to partake of what she'd prepared for us.

A tiled counter along the bathroom wall held a double sink and more luxurious toiletries, in case we'd forgotten anything. A glass, walk-in shower summoned from beyond the tub. It was a far cry from our hotel room in London, which was cramped, stale, and lacking in ambiance. I was especially touched by the soft music in the background.

"Who thought of that?" I wondered. "Brilliant!" It added such a magical, romantic touch to our experience. I loved all the thoughtful little additions. When I signed up with Mac's Adventures to coordinate our lodging in the Cotswolds, I expected basic accommodations, maybe two or three-star hotels. I definitely hadn't anticipated anything like this!

After we'd oohed and aahed and walked around the room gawking, we unpacked a few things. Then we ventured back across the courtyard to the main building and the front bar area, since it was too early for dinner. Feeling like we were in an historic pub, we settled into a window-seat in the corner and ordered gin and tonics. I thought how we really did fit into this English scene, since our drink was created when 19th century British soldiers and sailors in India began adding gin to tonic water to improve its taste. Apparently, the bitter tonic was mixed with gin and lime to make it more palatable.

We'd made reservations at the hotel's restaurant for 6 pm, so, when that time came, we went back to the lobby and were greeted at the dining room door by a waiter, who took us to our table. Since most Europeans don't eat dinner until 7 or 8 o'clock, we were the first to be seated at the far side of the room. Soon, another couple came in and sat at a nearby table. As we looked over the menu, I detected a southern accent and overheard them talking about Nashville, Tennessee. After a few minutes, I turned around and asked if they lived there.

"Yes," they nodded.

"My sister lives there," I said. "And we visit her and her family often. We love that area."

The conversation progressed to travel, and the husband, also named Mike, and his wife, Rosemary, explained their passion for waterfalls and how they loved to view the most spectacular ones they could find. They'd traveled to places like Belgium, Norway, Switzerland, and Iceland just to see the breathtaking beauty of falling water. Tomorrow they'd visit some in the Cotswolds, including ones in Broadway, Snowshill, and Upper Slaughter. After hearing their descriptions, I wished we had the time to experience these too.

"Oh well," I thought. "Maybe on another trip." Later I looked at pictures online, and the falls near Broadway and Snowshill looked especially magnificent.

They asked what drew us to hike around the Cotswolds, and I told them about my walk on the Camino and how it had inspired me to start a Facebook group for Senior Travelers on the Camino and, now, another site called Senior Travelers and Trekkers. We shared our information, and I friended them on Facebook. Rosemary was suffering from tinnitus and vertigo, and I thought about the people I'd met in Spain who were walking on the Camino to find healing. I also remembered Sandra at the airport, whose leg we prayed for. I said a silent prayer for Rosemary, and, in my journal that night, I wrote, "Lord, bless them both, and heal her!"

After a wonderful meal, we waddled back across the courtyard to our waiting boudoir. I sighed as we entered the room again and heard the classical music in the background. I noticed that, besides the soft musical strains, the bed was turned down, special chocolates were placed on the pillows, and a romantic light spread from a lamp in the corner to welcome us back. I loved this place!

It shouldn't have been difficult to drift peacefully into a sweet sleep as I lay beneath that warm, plush comforter in this comfortable bed with the pleasant music playing as I listened to the quiet night sounds. I thought about all the unexpected things we'd encountered that day: Sinikka at Paddington Station, the couple from Virginia, the man on the road to Moreton-in-Marsh who confirmed our way to the hotel, the amazing room and food at the hotel, and the friendly couple from Nashville. For these, I was very thankful.

But, gnawing in the back of my mind was the thought that we would start our trek the next day, and rain was in the forecast. It was the third week in May and, apparently, the continuation of a rainy season here.

"Oh, Lord," I prayed as I lay there, "help us to get through tomorrow and the rest of the week. I don't know what to expect or how we'll handle things but show us how to manage whatever comes our way."

It was a good prayer, and I'm glad I prayed it, considering what lay ahead.

Lesson Four

When in need, ask for help!

The helpful ladies at The Queen's Head Inn

"Listen to your body, and ask for help if you need it. Joy might come from not 'mastering' the trek, but stopping to experience a moment you hadn't planned to rest."—Sally Clark Deykerhoff

Our day started out happy with plates full of poached egg and smoked salmon covered with hollandaise sauce atop toasted English muffins. Yum! We slugged down as much hot coffee as we could manage since, when we stepped out of our door into the courtyard, the weather was cooler than expected, and we had to dodge multiple raindrops. I'd layered my clothing, as I learned to do while walking on the Camino. And I made sure to put on my hooded waterproof coat that extended to my knees after pulling on my water-resistant shoes and covering my backpack with a waterproof cover.

Suitcases packed and pulled across the courtyard through the rain before breakfast, we left them by the receptionist desk. A transfer company would pick them up and transport them to our next destination, The Slaughters Country Inn in Lower Slaughter. Outside the front door of the hotel at 8:30, our stomachs full from the hearty breakfast, we stood under an eave and gazed out at the dreary, pouring rain.

I noticed a short, white-haired woman standing next to us, peering out through the drops. Mike had nudged me when he noticed her at breakfast, sitting near our table.

"You should talk to her," he'd whispered. "Maybe she's walking too." I didn't feel compelled to start a conversation, thinking it was too early for some people, who like the morning quiet, so I shook my head.

"Are you walking?" I ventured now, seeing her waterproof gear and umbrella.

"Yes," she answered succinctly.

"So are we. To Lower Slaughter."

"I'm going to Stow-on-the-Wold, on the way to Lower Slaughter. I'm meeting friends there," she explained. "They chose to stay in a different place and are going another route."

"Where are you from?"

"California. Near Oakland. And you?"

"We're from a town in Missouri. Near Kansas City. What's your name?"

"Joanna. Should we go?" She cut me off with a definite message that she wanted to avoid any chit chat or overt friendliness and tackle the trek, despite the drizzle. She popped her bright blue umbrella open and got ready to cross the street. "We can find the trail together." And she promptly set out.

"Ok." I looked over at Mike, and we followed her steps. My online map, with a tracking arrow, pointed across the street then up a perpendicular road. Joanna was heading that way, so our directions were confirmed.

"It's always nice to find others walking the same route so you can verify that you're going the right way," I thought, "even if they're not super sociable."

Online maps like ours from Mac's can be very helpful, but we found them challenging at times. Sometimes the arrow would point one way then switch to another way. This was especially confusing when the path wasn't marked, and you came to a fork in the trail with no sign or clear indication of which way to go. Several times, we had to backtrack when the arrow showed to go one way but then alerted us we were headed in the wrong direction! We had to retrace valuable steps when Mike's legs were hurting, and my patience was very thin. That was not fun. Arg!

We passed a pretty stone-fence-lined lake before entering a path through a pasture. The drizzle was constant, and I looked ahead to see Joanna's blue umbrella bobbing along as she walked ahead of us. Covered from head to toe in black water-repellent gear, a backpack hanging in front, her white hair really stood out. I watched her for a while to make sure we followed in her footsteps. Since Mike's pace is much slower than mine, I soon caught up with her on the narrow path. I walked beside her for a while and tried to converse, as I did with so many hiking alone on the Camino. I had found many people walking by themselves open and eager to meet others and share stories. It was almost expected. I hoped for the same experience here.

"Maybe her abruptness at the hotel was a fluke," I thought. "She just doesn't know us very well!" I would give her another chance. Surely, she would want some company on this long, isolated trail.

She did open up to tell me a little about her past as a teacher. For this I was thankful. Now she was retired and traveling with friends. Her best buddy had moved to Idaho, she said. As a single person, she missed her friend, but, she made it clear, "I would never think of moving to a 'red' state, where the politics and people are very different."

"Hmmm." I thought about my own state and how it was a mix of many kinds of people, but mostly considered a "red," or conservative-leaning, state. It seemed sad that she would never consider living in a beautiful place like mine, just because the people might be dissimilar from her. This kind of boxed-in thinking was so strange to me, especially after crossing northern Spain with many kinds of folks from all over the planet. In fact, every walk of life combed the same territory in a combined effort.

We walked through sheep and crop-filled pastures, climbing over fences with steps when we needed to get into the next field. I let Joanna go ahead when I had to find a secluded place to relieve myself and perused the landscape for trees and bushes. I also wanted to wait for Mike to catch up with me

53

since he'd fallen behind as we talked. We'd gone almost three miles. At home, this would have taken us little more than an hour. Here, with the uneven terrain, the meadows broken up by fences to unlatch or climb over, and the winding dirt paths, it took us much longer.

Mike and I trekked, still in the rain, through more green pastures until we passed through a gate onto a paved road that led into a town called Longborough. I spotted signs for a village shop that served coffee, and I watched for it as we walked down a long street past many slate-roofed, honey-stone buildings and homes, some covered with white-flowered vines.

One rain-washed street with rows of charming townhomes faced a limestone brick wall on the other side topped with greenery that dripped down the wall's side. It reminded me of a tall, towering ice cream cone with mounds of pistachio ice cream on top. A dirt road lined with a low yellow-brick wall led from the street to a medieval-looking church with a square turret topped with crenellations and cross-topped pillars. A bright blue clock told time from the front of the turret, and, above that, ventilated windows indicated it might be a bell tower. Gargoyles thrust out their ugly faces above the windows.

Beside the road to the church, tilting tombstones stood in a row in the parish's manicured lawn. I wondered how old the church and the tombstones were, but we didn't take the time to stop and see. We just wanted to find a dry place to rest and shake off the morning's damp chill before venturing on.

I gazed down one street and spotted a sign for the Longborough Village Shop. Beside the shop, an A-frame read *"Open,"* and, beneath the announcement, it said, *"I thought of writing a fish joke, but I'm trying to scale back."* The words surrounded the picture of a fish. Beside the quirky sign, a rack held trays of free fresh vegetables. And I knew they'd have fresh coffee and pastries inside. We were greeted by two women and a man, who turned out to be from the States. After passing a counter topped with cake and pastries, we found a table by a window and removed our dripping backpacks and coats, draping them over an empty wooden chair. I immediately found a restroom upstairs and was supremely happy.

We ordered the spice cake with walnuts and maple frosting and frothy cappuccinos, and we were not disappointed. Delicious! As we sipped our warm drinks, we talked to the man, a longtime Pittsburgh resident who'd moved to Longborough because of a woman. We asked how he'd adjusted to life in a small, foreign village, especially since he was from a large, industrial city, and he said, without hesitation, that he loved it! We listened to his explanations and what he appreciated about life here. To us, it seemed like an idyllic place—it was quiet, the people were friendly, and they were surrounded by so much beauty in the buildings and pastoral scenery.

Working in this shop was one reason he enjoyed life in Longborough. The co-op, run by several volunteers from town, brought them all a great deal of camaraderie. Besides serving coffee and pastries to passers-by and locals, it was stocked with merchandise and food products. I think that a large part of their business came from tourists like us who happened to wander in while walking through the Cotswolds.

As we sat and watched the rain create large, round droplets on the windowpanes, two middle-aged Swiss women sat down next to us. They were also trekking through the countryside and going in the same direction as we were. We talked briefly, since they were in a hurry to keep going after they slugged down their coffee and gobbled their spice cake. We ran into them several more times that week in other Cotswold villages.

I would have liked to have gotten to know them better and find out what they'd discovered on their trek and why they'd decided to do it, but they always seemed to be in a hurry to get to the next place.

As it turned out, our stop at the Longborough Village Shop ended up being sorely needed, especially when we encountered what I consider the most challenging part of our journey. It was a bolster before the upcoming storm!

The road out of town wound around until we were traipsing through the countryside again, still in the drizzle, but, this time, through a wooded area. After climbing over a fence, we entered an ominous area with no plausible way through. We looked at each other and then at the trail. The seven or eight-foot-wide "path" was enclosed by fences and completely filled with feet-deep mud rutted with tracks from farm equipment. The grooves, filled with thick brown water, looked like treacherous little trenches. Mud jutting up around the ruts formed the entire path from one fence-forbidding side to the other with no way of escape. The only path was through it. No other options. The map showed this was *the only public walking route.*

Soooo, I moved one shaky foot forward and placed it precariously on the highest mud mound I could see and pushed down. My foot immediately sank deep into what felt like oozing quicksand and kept going down, down, down! I tried to lift it back out, pulling my leg back up with all my strength. Well, my foot finally came out of the slurping mess, but not my shoe! Now I teetered from side to side, with my arms extended, trying to keep my balance, holding my socked foot up in the air.

"For the love of God!" I yelled. I wasn't sure what to do next. *"Help!"*

No able to maintain my equilibrium any longer, my foot plunged back down into the sucking sludge! Trying to find the "bottom," I pushed down until the guzzling clag was up to my shin. Then I reached over to try to recover my shoe. As I did, I lost my balance completely, and I fell forward into the guzzling mire. Pushing my hands down to my midarms into the muck, I tried to get back up. I gradually stood, using my bent knees to push myself up, since my hands couldn't brace against the oozing stuff. My shoed foot was now deeply entrenched, and my socked foot was also completely sucked in. *"Holy crap!"* I couldn't help yelling.

At that moment, as I was pulling myself up from the slime, I glanced back to see how Mike was handling this disaster. Well, he wasn't. Waving his arms around like a crazed banshee, he was trying to balance on the foot that was stuck in the mud. He circled the other foot in the air along with his arms and desperately tried to reach for a nearby branch. He grabbed onto one, but, like me, he finally lost his battle with the sucking muck, and the other foot went down with a splattering plop to be drawn deep down into the bog. Now, he was slowly moving toward me, one slurpy, sinking step after another, as I also tried to maneuver forward. I'm sure we looked like heaving, mud-covered earth creatures making our way.

I thought that "Slogging-through-the-Mud" would be the perfect name for the nearest village!

We were super relieved to see an opening in the fence ahead with a grassy area beyond it. Whew! We slogged our way to it and gratefully came up to a level, solid dirt path. As we stood there, we couldn't help laughing as we looked at each other. I was covered from my neck down with thick, brown globs. I leaned over, still laughing, and pulled a gooey, mud-filled shoe back onto my muck-soaked, socked foot. Mike was not entirely covered, since he hadn't fallen in, but his lower half was still caked with crud. We definitely looked like the mud monster in the Scooby Doo cartoons. Of course, we took pictures of ourselves and cackled whenever we looked at the photos or told the grueling story about our slog through the sludge in the Cotswolds.

My main concern was my phone. I reached into my raincoat pocket and drew it out. Thank God it had a cover on it. The cover was crusty, but the phone was in good shape. It was hard not to get mud on it, though, when I touched it.

Past a pasture, we came to a fenced-in farm. And there, beside the railing, stood a bucket and a faucet with a hose attached. Someone must have known we were coming or seen this scene before! Without hesitation, I turned on the spigot, lifted the hose, and started spraying. I took off one shoe—the one attached to my mud-soaked sock—and I sprayed the inside to remove most of the muck. Then I began on my pants. They just soaked up the water like a sponge, but at least the crud came off. Then I started on my coat. I removed most of the slimy stuff, but I was still filthy and freezing cold! It was in the 50s, and even my layers of shirts and fleece couldn't completely block out the cold. I shivered and shook as I rejoined the path after my hose shower. At least I wasn't dripping mud now. Hopefully the water would dry a little before we entered the hotel lobby in Lower Slaughter.

I could envision the looks we'd get as we entered the pristine lobby of a beautiful hotel, looking like we'd crawled out of a medieval forest where we'd been hibernating, covered with muck and smelling like mildew and mold. The receptionist would take one look at us, sternly frown, trying to hide his or her disgust, then summarily sneer and ask, "Can I help you?" with an upper-crust English accent.

"How embarrassing!" I thought. "Lord, would You give us some grace and help the hotel staff to be kind and understanding?" I wondered if they might have seen other Cotswold trekkers who'd traipsed through the rain and mud to show up in a similar condition.

"God, I hope so!" I shook from the cold and imagined contempt. *"It is what it is!"* I said out loud, now my favorite saying.

Dripping, we made our way around the farm over a road that circled the property, but then we wondered if we were going the right way. There were no "Public Access" signs to show us which way to go, and my app wasn't making it very clear. Two women stood brushing two large horses in a barn nearby, and I thought of stopping to ask them where to get onto the public path. But as we turned toward the barn, up walked the Swiss women from the Longborough Village Shop. They were gazing at a physical map and a phone, and they looked as confused as we were about which way to go.

"What do you think?" I asked as I approached them.

"We're not sure. But we think it's this way." They turned toward the road we'd just come from. We hesitatingly followed them since my directions weren't clear either. The little arrow on my online map pointed one way, but, as we walked, it turned another way. On the other side of the farm, they chose to follow a road downhill. As we stood there, trying to decipher my directions, a bearded local man, wearing a blue slicker with the hood over his baseball cap and carrying a hiking pole, walked up. Later, I wondered if God had sent him in much the same way He'd brought us Sinikka at Paddington Station and the man at the river park in Windsor. It was such a strange coincidence that he happened to step up at that very moment. And on a road out in the middle of nowhere!

I didn't hesitate to ask, "Do you know which way to Stow-in-the-Wold?" This was our next stop on the way to Lower Slaughter.

"Well," he said. "You can go down that road," he pointed to the road the Swiss women were headed down. "Or, if you go straight," he gestured ahead, "you'll find a path across a field that is a shortcut to Stow-on-the-Wold, which is at the bottom of that hill. It's a much shorter route."

We thanked him profusely for his advice and decided to take the shorter route, even though it was not even an option in our directions.

"Trust a local," I thought, "more than your phone."

I was quickly learning that you can save a lot of time and effort if you'll just ask friendly locals for help. We were especially thankful when this recommended path took us over a paved walk bordered by a picturesque stone fence, through a rustic wooden gate, and past a pasture filled with the most unusual white-footed, black sheep with white stripes from their foreheads to their shiny black noses. I had never seen sheep like these before. They reminded me of the nursery rhyme I'd heard so many times as a child: *"Baa, baa black sheep, have you any wool."* One came over to the fence and smiled at me, grinning through his black lips and squinting his little brown eyes up at mine as if to say, "Who-o-o are you and wher-r-r-e are you from? By the way, do you have anything we can eat?" He made my day! And I was so glad we'd taken this more obscure, local route.

We passed through another gate that led to a highway and trudged on toward Stow-on-the-Wold. As we drew closer, Mike informed me that during our memorable mud-battle, when he grabbed the branch to avoid falling, he'd seriously twisted his knee and pulled a leg muscle. This particular muscle happened to be the same one he'd injured as a teen, when he attempted to water ski, only to end up doing a side-to-side split—an interesting move where his legs spread out sideways. This extraordinary gymnastic feat happened while he was trying to maneuver his way up to the top of the water on his skis as the boat zoomed forward. Needless to say, that leg muscle was still vulnerable, even at age 81. Being old is no joke, I was learning, and any physical mishap can prove pretty hazardous if you don't take it seriously and consider your vulnerabilities.

I felt badly for him, and we decided to look for a place to stop and rest for a while. We'd call it a day and try to get a cab to our hotel in Lower Slaughter. We spotted a cross street into Stow-on-the-Wold from the busy road where we walked, and we made our way across and up a hill toward the center of town. Watching Mike hobble along, I craned my neck to spot a café, tavern, or restaurant that might be open as we inched our way up the winding road. Just as we rounded a bend, the market square unfolded before us. Honey-stone buildings and cobbled streets surrounded a triangular-shaped brick island bearing a tall pillar topped with a cross. It was early in the afternoon and still rainy, and the streets looked deserted, even though the shops looked charming and inviting. I wished that we had the time or energy to explore this magical place. But our urgent need was to find a place willing to seat and serve us. As I turned the corner, lo and behold, directly in front of us hung a sign on a building that read "Queen's Head Inn," and people were going inside. *It was open!*

We soon discovered that the real town charm of Stow-in-the-Wold was the people. Though we trudged sloppily into the tavern, we were welcomed warmly. It was a busy place. Even on a rainy weekday afternoon, the tables were full of locals. I noticed three older residents sitting in a corner with their beers foaming temptingly in front of them. Enough light streamed through a multi-paned window behind them that I could see their expressions as they leaned toward each other, obviously sharing the local gossip. Dark wooden beams framed the rain-soaked panes, and deer antlers pierced their points toward the low ceiling, reminding everyone of past deer hunts. Beside the window, a brass corn-popper and a pewter plate hung from the limestone brick wall, prompting memories of times gone by.

Two cheerful ladies behind the bar hailed us. One was in her 20s—bouncy, chestnut-brown-haired, and a ball of happy helpfulness. Her name was Eva. Kirstie was a taller, heavier-set, long-haired blond in her 30s. Neither were bothered at all by our disheveled appearance or our slimy, mud-covered coats and shoes. They seemed familiar with walkers like us barging in when it was raining. We ordered drinks at the bar as we gazed at an overhead brown wood-beam that announced: "Donnington Cotswold Ales." A line of pewter beer mugs hung, shining, from the sign.

The pub reminded me of another adventure we'd had in Ireland in 2003, when we'd rented a car with another couple and driven to the town of Dingle. During a breakneck drive through the Dingle Peninsula, over one-lane roads with protruding bushes on one side and a 100-foot drop over a cliff on the other, we prayed for our lives. The riskiest trick was facing oncoming traffic when there was no place to pull over. Thankfully, we were almost alone on that road. After the hair-raising ride, we decided we needed to stop at a Dingle pub, and we chose John Benny's, where we sat on chairs and a cushioned window seat and sipped foamy Irish beer and looked out at a beautiful harbor view. We were surprised when an older local man came over and sat with us. He proceeded to tell us the history of Dingle, and he didn't skip a detail as he elaborated on all the movies filmed in the area, including *The Quiet Man* with John Wayne and Maureen O'Hara. He also expounded on all the things that made the town famous. As a boat tour guide, he loved his work. That was obvious from all the interesting stories of locals and tourists he told. And we enjoyed every moment with him. So much so that we hated to leave, but we had to rejoin our group in Killarney. This was our first exposure to the friendly Irish, and now, in the Cotswolds, I thought the people seemed to have the same wonderful, amiable geniality.

I asked to use the restroom at the Queen's Head Inn so I could wash up the best I could. Pointed toward it, I slid inside to wipe off my coat and pants and try to get the imbedded crud out of my fingernails. Back in the bar area, we sat discreetly on the edges of high wooden stools at a table near the counter. We tried not to leave a muddy film behind us as we sipped our drinks, and we hoped we didn't look too outrageous to these kind Cotswolders. It was too late for lunch and too early for dinner, so we chewed on some bars from the bottom of my backpack, along with some bar chips. As we sat there, I asked Eva how we could get a cab. My phone was down to a 20 percent charge now, and we definitely didn't want to go back out in the drizzling rain or try to trek the rest of the way to Lower Slaughter, especially after sipping drinks and enjoying sitting in the warm pub. She plugged in my phone for me and said that it was hard to get cabs to come here, since there wasn't a lot of traffic between this town and the next. A man standing near us offered to call his friend who drove a cab, and he stepped outside to make the call. Eva warned us that he was not very trustworthy, and she directed me to a posted list of cab drivers. With my phone partially charged now, I tried a few of the numbers, but none of the calls would go through. A couple sitting nearby tried to help by making suggestions on how to make a call in the UK. I found out that, within the country, calls use a different code than if they are made between the US and the UK. Still with no success, I turned to Eva, she offered to call for me, and she was able to reach a driver who agreed to come. While we finished up our drinks, we chatted with her and Kirstie, and I asked if I could take their picture and post it online. They happily said yes and were excited that they might be famous! Before we walked outside to wait for our cab, we hugged the two women good-bye. By the time the driver came, we'd befriended several of the people in the tavern.

We found out later that the red-headed queen on the "Queen's Head Inn" sign was none other than Elizabeth I, and this historic 1600s-era tavern has been described as "a near perfect example of a small Cotswold town pub" by *Pub Gallery*. I thought about how, so many times, we'd "just happen" to land in these unique places that ended up being memorable, and then we'd discover they were very sought-after destinations. When I later rewatched Rick Steve's episode on West England, I realized that he highlighted this pub when he visited Stow-on-the-Wold.

I also discovered that the name of the town is derived from the Old English words "stow" and "wold." Stow comes from the Saxon word for "religious meeting place," and wold means "rolling hill," according to *Stow Civic Society*. When combined, the name roughly means "holy place on the hill." It's the highest town in the Cotswolds at 800 feet above sea level, and it encapsulates the area with a large market square, limestone buildings, narrow lanes, shops, cafés, restaurants, pubs, and tea rooms. I regretted that we didn't have more time here, especially after our welcoming reception at the Queen's Head Inn.

Our driver came, and we were very thankful to have a ride with this nice Kenyan man in his super-clean van. I think he regretted agreeing to pick us up though. As we stood, ready to climb in with our dirty coats, pants, and shoes, he gave us sideways glances and quickly grabbed some towels from the back to cover the seats. I didn't blame him!

We found out later, from a cabby in Oxford, that in the UK, especially in London, taxi drivers must fork out considerable expense to be eligible. After the upfront fees for licensing, applications, and insurance (about £2,000), they must also buy a car. The annual operating cost is about £24,000 a year. No wonder this cabby, who'd made a life-changing move here from Kenya, and paid so much to start a business, would want to protect his precious van from two mud-slinging tourists who needed a ride.

Despite our filthy clothing, he was kind enough to drive us to The Slaughters Country Inn, which ended up being a grand 2.9 miles away! The name "Slaughter" in Upper and Lower Slaughter comes from the Old English word "slohtre," which means "muddy place" or "place of pools."

"How appropriate is that?" I chuckled, considering our walk that day.

We drove up to what looked like a large, well-maintained country estate. The first thing I noticed as we approached was a large, circular, moss-covered stone planter full of green, purple, and pink plants. I wondered how old it was. The inn's buildings were all built with the honey-limestone, and most

65

were draped with vines. Lead-paned windows surrounded by greenery decorated one building, and a stairway climbed mysteriously from the courtyard to an outside door on the second floor of another.

An inviting wooden door with a slate-roofed entryway led to the bar. Lanterns on either side hung ready to be lit, when the evening dimmed to darkness, so visitors could find their way inside or make their way outside to their cars after a nightcap. Two planters with bushy plants stood beside the door and, above it, a hanging sign read "The Slaughters." Beneath the Old English lettering, two funny-looking men were pictured wearing medieval floppy hats, white shapeless coats (or dresses?), one with a red scarf around his neck, and both wearing high, black boots. They sat on stools at a table, lifting their mugged beers into the air. And I wondered who they were supposed to be. Below the picture, the sign said, "Comfort Food, Real Ales & Fine Wines." A mat sat in front of the worn door, welcoming visitors into the cozy interior.

The inn entryway, just beyond the bar entrance, invited similarly with a lantern over a wooden door. A welcome mat also sat in front, but, as we exited the van and thanked our kind driver, I wondered just how welcome we'd be! Here we were, dirty and stinking of deteriorating debris and moldering mud, walking into a five-star hotel.

"Dreadful! *How embarrassing!*" I turned to Mike. And he winced, knowing exactly how I felt. But we had no choice. In we tromped, backpacks attached to our filthy backs, trudging up to the front desk.

My guess is that the lovely receptionists, who greeted us warmly, had seen this before, because, like the women at the pub, they didn't blink an eye. They just smiled kindly. It was almost 3 pm, and our room was ready, so one of the ladies walked us up some carpeted steps to show us to our room. We both tiptoed. When she opened the door, I was impressed. Not quite as spacious as our room at The White Hart Royal Hotel, it was just as accommodating. Muted light streamed through a large multi-paned picture window on one wall. Two comfortable chairs sat below the window, and a desk and chair occupied a corner. A bureau faced the king-sized bed that beckoned to us. And, through a door, light poured from a small upper window in a large bathroom with a toilet, a warming radiator and rack, and a gleaming white tub where we could wash our filthy clothes.

"Yes!" I whispered to myself.

The hotel didn't have a laundry service. None of the hotels we encountered in the Cotswolds did. So, we had to handwash and hang dry what needed laundering. I immediately set to work stripping off layers of clothing. My coat came off first, then my shoes, socks, and pants. As I leaned over the large tub, I meticulously washed each item to remove every bit of imbedded debris. It took me at least an hour to wash mine, then Mike started on his. I was thankful that, in most English bathrooms, there's a rack above the radiator where you can hang wet clothing to dry. In our case, we draped our wet clothes over every surface in the bathroom. Since we'd need to wear our socks again in the next couple of days (I only brought three pairs), and the wool ones might need more time to dry, we hung them on the radiator rack.

This process took up the rest of the afternoon. We ended the ordeal by taking long, hot showers. *"Yes!"* again. I washed my hair, put on some warm clothes, and got ready to go downstairs. I was especially happy I'd purchased the thick sweater at the market in Moreton-in-Marsh. It felt cozy and warm on this cool evening. Our dinner reservation was for 6 pm, and it was 5, so we wandered around the grounds, taking pictures of the vine-covered stone buildings and the spacious green lawn behind the inn. Then we headed to the bar for the "Comfort Food, Real Ales & Fine Wines."

We found the food at The Slaughters Country Inn truly wonderful. That night, we treated ourselves to beef fillets, mashed potatoes with truffles, and asparagus. It couldn't have tasted better! For dessert, we had caramel soufflé with ice cream and sauce. Amazing! As I savored the soufflé, I thought about how we'd survived this day. And I was thankful. But I wondered what we'd encounter the next day. What would the paths be like? Would we have to slog through more mud?

"Surely not!" I cringed and quickly tried to think about more positive things, like my dessert.

Mac's reservations allowed for a "free" day, with another night's stay here at The Slaughters. We could use it to wander into nearby Bourton-on-the-Water, less than two miles away. This idea sounded great to us both. Rather than trek a longer way, we'd opt for this shorter walk. Mike's knee and leg were still sore, so we needed to take it easy.

For now, we appreciated the ambiance of this charming restaurant with window views of an inviting greenspace lined with wooden benches. And, as I sat there gazing out, I recounted all the helpers we'd met that day: Joanna, who confirmed that we were going the right way, the mysterious man on the road who showed us a shorter and easier path, the ladies at Queen's Head Inn, the van driver, and the welcoming staff at this hotel.

We were also learning how important it is to ask for help when we needed it! And not to feel like we had to know how to do everything exactly right the first time. Such an important lesson!

Now, I wondered, would we find more helpers on our way tomorrow if we needed them? And, knowing us, we probably *would* need them!

Lesson Five

Appreciate kindness

Kind Kate drives us to Bourton-on-the-Water

"In England we were eight hours early for a ferry. I decided to sleep outside in my sleeping bag next to a graveyard. I was awoken (startled) at sunrise by a lovely old lady with a cup of tea. She must've thought I was homeless. How incredible kindness is!"—Rob Lucjak

Our raincoats were dry! Yay! Since we were here for two nights, we hoped the rest of our clothing would be dry by the next day.

"Thank God for an extra day!" I said to myself.

At breakfast, I happily inhaled another hefty English breakfast and was thankful for the unlimited coffee. But Mike looked down at his smoked salmon and eggs, and I could tell something was bothering him. After I pressed, he confessed that slogging through the constant rain the day before and then hurting his leg as he negotiated the challenging craggy path had made him feel discouraged about walking today. He was still a bit tired and the muscle behind his leg was very tender. But he was determined to try again.

"It's harder for an 81-year-old to recuperate from a strain than a 71-year-old," I had to remind myself. This confirmed our decision to go the shorter route into nearby Bourton-on-the-Water. In the room, after breakfast, I said a short prayer, "Lord, help Mike! His leg is better, but he needs to be easy on it. Thanks for giving him strength!"

We started our walk at 9:30 am and discovered St. Mary's church in Lower Slaughter very close by. The church's building and roof are made of Cotswold stone, and it boasts an awe-inspiring tower. According to the *Lower Slaughter Parish Council*, the interior dates from the 13th century, but the exterior was rebuilt in 1867 by Charles Shapland Whitmore in the early English style. A wooden gate opened onto a beautifully-landscaped lawn enclosed by greenery-draped stone walls that led up to a covered gated entry by the church. We didn't go inside, but we appreciated seeing the sumptuous surrounding grounds.

Across the road from the church, we followed a trail along a stream traversed by a cement bridge, and we appreciated the tall, yellow daylilies that lined the path. Across the rippling brook, we could see the grounds of The Slaughters Country Inn—immaculately kept and adorned with welcoming wooden benches near the water. Farther down the dirt path, a bright yellow-flower-dotted pasture spread out to accommodate groups of horses and cows who grazed blissfully. Our trail morphed into a road farther down, and my map didn't clearly indicate which way to go from here. We walked toward a busy highway called Stow Road with no clear path in sight, so we went up a muddy road that went off to the right. It dead-ended at a brewery called Hawkstone, where a huge open tent full of tables and chairs sat to one side of a large building.

Being the adventuress that I imagine myself to be, I ventured into the tent, hoping to find someone. Mike lagged behind, wondering where I was going and why. Sure enough, at the far side of the tent, I spotted a man standing behind an open bar. Having learned not to hesitate to ask for directions, I walked right up to him and asked how to get to Bourton-on-the-Water. He pointed back the way we'd just come.

"Go down to the light, then turn left," was all he said.

Thankful for any help we could get, but not understanding completely what he meant, we retraced our steps back over the muddy road. This time we noticed a meadow full of adorable white sheep behind some bushes. After oohing and aahing, we found the light on the highway as we emerged from the road and faced the highway. We crossed, as we'd understood him to say, then turned left and trekked over a rough, narrow trail beside a highway as cars and trucks whizzed past us. We saw no sign of a town, and I just knew we were heading the wrong way.

"For the love of God," I muttered and thought of another memorable time when we got lost while wandering aimlessly through the narrow streets in Marrakech.

It was March 2019, and we were enjoying an eventful trip to Morocco but quickly finding out that it's easy get lost in the alleyways, or souks, that spread out like fingers from the main square in the town's medina quarter. With over 9,000 narrow side streets that connect shops, homes, businesses, schools, and mosques, it would be easy to get disoriented and never find your way out of the maze. After trying to keep track of where we'd been and where we were now, we were somehow able to retrace our steps and find our way back to the main square. *Whew!* Being surrounded by many people having no familiarity with our language was, needless-to-say, super scary, especially when we lost our way. The experience was frightening, but, at the same time, fascinating. We were easily entranced, and sidetracked, by the men in traditional Moroccan clothing, leading mules pulling carts piled high with local produce. And the small enclaves, where men worked tirelessly keeping ovens lit and glowing by throwing more wood inside a furnace, as local women brought unbaked bread for him to cook. And the many rows of shops, where vendors offered handmade pottery and scarves and textiles and shoes and dried fruit and carpets and lanterns and bowls of many-colored spices. Everything felt so exotic and unique, and so different from life in our town.

And then, I remembered the time, in 2006, when we were on the island of Rhodes on a Greek Isle cruise. After being awed by the Palace of the Grand Master of the Knights, we ended up walking into the middle of a busy thoroughfare with streets full of tourist shops. One drew us in, and we somehow got separated, though I stood in the same place the whole time! I was engrossed in some knickknacks on a shelf, trying to decide what trinkets I needed to add to my collections and commemorate this visit. When I finally finished my internal debate and decided to pass on all of them, since I really didn't need more paraphernalia, I looked around the store and couldn't see Mike anywhere. I walked outside and stood in the middle of the paved passageway and gazed up and down at the rows of shops. He was nowhere to be found. I waited there, hoping he might spot me, but time was ticking, and, after about 15 minutes, I realized that I had exactly 20 minutes to get back to the ship before it sailed without me. I panicked. Deciding that he was on his own to make it back, I hightailed it past the shops and searched for any sign of him. Out of the busy market area, I spotted the harbor and our ship in the distance. And I walked as fast as I could through an ugly industrial area, past workers and docked boats, feeling conspicuous and vulnerable as I strolled through a foreign place alone, not knowing what the views of a woman walking by herself were here. Finally, after covering the distance in record time, I boarded the ship, huffing and puffing, and I worried whether or not Mike would make it back before we sailed. I stormed down the narrow passageway to our room, feeling frustrated, irritated, and concerned at the same time. I unlocked the door, muttering to myself, and, as I entered the room, I looked up and *there was Mike!* I was at the same time relieved and angry, so I uttered a few choice words.

"Where have you *been?*" As I spat the words out through gritted teeth, my voice raised a few notches. "I looked *everywhere* for you?"

"I couldn't find *you!*" he spoke incredulously. "*I* looked everywhere! And I finally came back to the ship!"

"*Wha-a-a-t!*" Now my voice was really raised. "*I never left the spot I was in!*"

That was before cell phones and being able to call someone to see where they were. Though neither of us were technically lost, somehow we'd missed each other in broad daylight! And I will never forget it.

At least now, being lost, we were in an English-speaking country. For this I was thankful! And suddenly, I spotted a gas station up ahead.

"I'm going to ask for help," I yelled back at Mike so he could hear me above the whooshing din of the speeding cars and trucks. And we somehow managed to get across the highway without getting hit. I could just imagine the headline in *The Cotswold Journal:* "Two lost, elderly Americans are flattened by oncoming traffic while stupidly crossing a busy highway." I cringed.

Just as we entered the station parking lot, I saw a parked tram with a sign on it that read, "The Villager." It looked like a local tourist bus, and I walked right up to it. A friendly-looking lady was sitting in the driver's seat. So, I leaned into the open doorway and asked her if we were going in the right direction to Bourton-on-the-Water.

"No!" she smiled. "It's the other way. You must go back down the way you came to a light, then bear left."

"Shoot! *Really?* We just walked all the way here from that light. My husband's leg is bothering him. Can we pay you for a ride?" I begged, trying to look as pitiful as possible.

"Well, I wasn't going in that direction. I was on my way to Stow-in-the-Wold. But I'd be happy to take you there," she smiled again. I loved this woman! And I became even more thankful for kind people.

"Thank you so much!" I was surprised at how quickly she'd changed her mind. "What can I pay you?"

"Donations only," she said and pointed at a bucket beside her. "I take people in need of transportation to places in this area."

I guess she thought we qualified!

"What a God-send!" I thought as I placed a handful of coins in the bucket and introduced ourselves to Kate as we hopped onto the tram. We found some seats, and she escorted us back up Stow Road, turned left at the light onto another street, and, within minutes, we were in Bourton-on-the-Water. Unbelievable! I thanked her profusely and we hopped off in front of The Willow, a pub and restaurant. We waved good-bye and made our way up the quaint and scenic High Street past a monument with a cross-topped pillar at the top of some steps. Then we trekked along a narrow river to look at the stone-supported bridges.

The name Bourton-on-the-Water comes from the Saxon words "burh," which means fortification or camp, and "ton," which means estate or village, according to *cotswold.gov.uk*. The town's location along the Windrush River made it an important site during the Roman era. In the heart of the Cotswolds, it's famous for five stone bridges that date from between 1654 and 1911 and give the village the nickname of "Venice of the Cotswolds." The monument on the square is a memorial commemorating the first and second world wars.

We entered Victoria Hall on High Street, where a craft show was underway. I met two ladies with displays and got their cards. One had a table full of handsome, handmade dolls and decorations. The other exhibited hand-stamped zippered bags of many shapes and sizes, along with towels and placemats. I took pictures of the smiling women and told them I'd post their pictures and products online. Outside, we ran into an older couple with three adorable dachshunds: one black with a brown muzzle, one blonde, and one mottled blond and brown. Of course, we had to stop and pet them! I have found that most people brave enough to take their dogs out in public are usually very open to strangers petting them. That's because they are so proud of "Pretzel" or "Waffles" or "Puddles," and they really believe that theirs is the cutest dog ever.

In our neighborhood at home, we've gotten to know many neighbors simply by walking our dogs around the block. People we never knew have emerged to become fast friends, especially if they have their own furry family members. Sadly though, in the States, many businesses, parks, and paths do not welcome dogs, which I find unfortunate, especially after traveling in Europe, where dogs are welcome everywhere, even in restaurants where children are sometimes not allowed. (I found it that way in Germany back in the 1960s while traveling.) I wonder if it's because Americans have a harder time controlling their dogs. Who knows? But, here in the Cotswolds, we saw dog-owners on every street corner, and we were happy to stop and pet them, since we missed our own fur babies at home.

After peeking through windows, and drooling over the pastry displays, we settled on The Chestnut Tree for lunch. It was busy, with a good selection of soups and sandwiches and pasties. I had always wanted to try a pasty, which is a folded pastry filled with seasoned meat, cheese, or vegetables and very popular in parts of England. So, I ordered a cheese and onion pasty, and Mike got a ham and cheese croissant. Yum! For dessert we had bread pudding with thick "clotted cream," also an English tradition. All washed down with the local Hawkstone Brewery beer, which I wanted to try, since we'd had a personal experience with the brewery's owner.

After lunch, we stopped at Mrs. Rolt's Tea Room, because it looked inviting and cozy. This was the only place we went on our trip that proved to be a mistake. A lady at the entry motioned for us to sit down but never returned to take our order. We finally got up to leave and, as we did, a family at a table near us also departed, frustrated by the lack of service. We ended up going back to The Willow, and I ordered a thick, hot, melt-in-your-mouth mocha drink. Mike got a cappuccino, and we shared a sparkling water. The young lady who served us was very attentive, which we appreciated after experiencing a definite lack of attention at the last place.

After savoring my drink, I approached the bar and asked about getting a cab or shuttle back to The Slaughters Country Inn. I was concerned about Mike's sore leg, and I didn't want to overdo the walking or get lost again going back. A kind young lady behind the bar named Amica offered to call for us, since I still couldn't get my calls to go through. She tried three times with no response from cab companies. Finally, she said, "I get off at 3 pm. Meet me in front of the restaurant at 10 minutes 'til 3, and I will walk you to the path to your hotel. It's close to where I live." She had to pick up her daughter at preschool on the way home but said it was no problem to walk with us and make sure we didn't get lost.

"*Wow!*" I said, my eyes wide. "Thank you so much for being willing to do that!" I was amazed by her eagerness to help two total strangers. And old ones at that!

It was a little past 1:30 now. We had over an hour to kill. Making our way down Sherborne Street, next to The Willow, we passed the Cotswold Motoring Museum, where a car sat out front covered with vines and a sign. I'm sure it was a very fascinating exhibition, but, not being car enthusiasts, we were more drawn to the quaint cottages farther down the street.

Made of Cotswold stone and surrounded by hedged gardens and low stone walls, the picturesque house-fronts were decorated with urns full of colorful flowers, and the multi-paned, leaded windows were draped with rose-colored vines. An arched door under a triangular portico invited special guests into one impressive building with stone-framed, paned windows and fanciful urns on the roof. It reminded me of a Dickens-era estate house, and I wondered how old it was. It was for sale, and I could only guess at the price. Farther down, another honey-stone home with a slate roof and two prominent chimneys was surrounded by an old but charming picket fence. The facade was covered with bushy green and red vines that engulfed the windows and hovered over the porticoed front door.

In front of one cottage, as I lingered, appreciating the views, an older gentleman walked by and struck up a conversation. Stuart appeared to be in his 80s, and he looked typically English in his flat paddy cap. He told me how his wife had recently passed away.

"I am so sorry." My face drooped when he told me, and I thought about my older relatives who had died recently. He then showed me all the veteran pins that decorated his coat pocket, and I tried to show some appreciation and admiration, since I knew he needed these. I think so many older folks feel lonely, especially if they live alone. They just yearn for company and conversation, but they may not be able to find either amid younger people, who are always in a hurry to get to the next place.

Stuart then said he was trying to downsize since his wife's death, and I asked how long he'd lived in Bourton-on-the-Water.

"All my life!" he exclaimed. He still loved the area. Everyone I met expressed the same feeling. I wondered how he felt about all the tourists who swarmed the streets.

"It slowed down during Covid," he explained. I had heard that from others. "But it's picked up again." He didn't seem dismayed by the recent activity. I don't know about the locals who live in the Cotswold towns, but I thought the businesses appreciated the visitors. Though I saw many coming from other countries, most of the people walking around the towns were from England.

Meeting this kind man made my day, and I wished him well just as Mike, who'd been taking pictures, joined us, and we turned to go. One more hike through town, and we arrived back at The Willow by 2:50 pm. As we sat at a picnic table in front of the restaurant waiting, we looked up to see the two Swiss women we'd met in Longborough walking past us. We greeted each other as if we were old friends.

"That's the beauty of traveling," I thought. "When you recognize anyone you've seen before, you feel a bit more at home in an unfamiliar place."

We followed Amica to the other side of the restaurant so she could go inside and retrieve a tricycle-stroller (a tricycle with a handle in back to push) for her daughter. As we approached the busy High Street through town, we were shocked to see a car screech to a stop in front of an elderly man and a young man lean out his car window to scream, *"Get out of the road, old man! What do you think you're doing? I almost hit you!"* The older gentleman had inadvertently wandered into the street at just the wrong moment and, seeing the oncoming traffic, he'd backed up quickly to the sidewalk near us. He was obviously flustered, and I felt very sorry for him. I thought about Mike or my dad as he aged and how this could have been them. It made me sad, amid all the kindness I'd witnessed today, to come across something so shockingly rude.

"How disrespectful!" I thought. I understood the frustration of the young man after almost hitting the old guy, but he also needed to slow down and allow for some mercy and thankfulness for *not* killing him. Maybe an apology to the older man for being in such a rush instead of hateful, angry accusations?

We walked alongside Amica across the street to a side road, where we picked up a walking path that was parallel to High Street. It led past backyards, open areas, and many old structures. After a couple of blocks, she entered a gate and went into a building to get Lily. Her sweet little two-year-old in hand, she returned through the gate, and we were joined by a bright-red-haired friend and her small daughter. Amica took Lily's jacket off but left her wearing a small pink backpack and holding her pink and blue lunch bag. She set her on the tricycle to pedal as she pushed the handle. Down two more blocks, we came to a park, where Amica's friend and her daughter, who'd gone ahead, greeted them at the entry. Amica handed her daughter off to them so she could walk us to the street, where we'd find our path to the inn. On the way, she showed us where she lived in a townhouse with a friend, close to her parents. I wondered about her life and her story, but never felt like I could ask. I was just thankful that she wanted to take this time to help us! Another unexplained but much appreciated kindness.

Soon we reached Stow Road, running perpendicular to High Street. It was then that we saw the traffic light in front of us and realized this was the one we'd come to before but ended up turning to go in the wrong direction. When we saw the yellow-flowered pasture of horses and cows in front of us, we immediately recognized the path that led to our hotel. I hugged Amica. I couldn't thank her enough for taking this time to show us the way back.

As we crossed Stow Road, I noticed a group of older women crossing at the intersection. As they passed by, I caught a glimpse of Joanna, but not in time to say hello to her. I think she recognized me, but, for some reason, didn't want to acknowledge us. It seemed odd. I wondered if she felt we were just too different for her liking, and she was embarrassed to introduce us to her friends. Again, this made me thankful for all the small kindnesses we'd experienced along the way, especially today.

We made it to our path, past the sheep and horses and cows, to our waiting room at The Slaughters Country Inn, where we showered, rested, then wandered down to the pub to talk about our day as we sipped gins and tonic before another lovely dinner.

We knew we'd experience more surprises on our trek the next day, but we had no idea what they'd be or who we might see. I wondered if we'd come across the Swiss travelers again or meet someone new. Would someone step up to help us if we got lost again? Like today. Or would we help others find their way? ("That would be a miracle!" I chuckled to myself.) So many questions. What should we expect? Only God knew.

Lesson Six

Focus on the good things

The unusual sheep near Winchcombe

"I would rather have aspirational expectations such as 'Embrace and be grateful for all I encounter.' This would give a positive attitude toward a rainy day for example. You would be surprised how embracing a rainy day turns it into a positive experience."—Dianne Clay

O ur clothes were dry by the next morning, just in time to pack up and go to our next stop, Winchcombe. Mike decided that he wanted to try to walk as far as he could today. He didn't want to completely throw in the

83

towel...yet! As we sat appreciating another wonderful breakfast, we recalled our conversation the morning before. Two evenings ago, after the challenging, rain-soaking mud-walk, he had pulled a waiter at the restaurant over to show him how he couldn't fit his long legs under the table because of the way the table legs were situated. In retrospect, this may have been the final straw for him, since his leg was very sore. He'd even pulled other customers into his complaint. The whole ordeal had bothered me, because my goal for this trip was to bless people we came in contact with and show them that not ALL Americans are demanding and rude. I was always looking for "doors" into conversations with those I met to share the joy and peace and hope I had because of my faith. But this! *It made me mad!*

After dinner, in the room, I'd confronted him, since I was unable to contain my irritation. Mike had apologized for grumbling and confessed that he was feeling "down" about the constant rain and his leg. He probably also wasn't thrilled about having to wash so many clothes after the demanding slog. He was tired, he admitted. That night, he couldn't sleep. He'd lain awake, asking God to forgive his bad attitude. He wanted to be more thankful. The next morning, over breakfast, he apologized.

"I don't want to be that way," he looked down sadly.

"I understand," I said. Then, as we ate, "I think that in every situation, you have a choice," I reflected. "You can look for what's good and what you appreciate, which is hard when you're confronted by pain and you're overly tired. Or you can choose to see only the negatives and focus on what you don't like—the terrible things."

I thought about a quote from Max Lucado I'd read in his devotional, *God is With You Everyday*: "Life comes with voices. Voices lead to choices. Choices have consequences."

Mike was in total agreement. And now, at the start of a new day, we purposely recalled all the wonderful and kind people who had stepped up to help us the day before. People who didn't have to help us but chose to. And we were thankful for how God had worked so many things out for us so that we were in the right place at the right time to receive the help we needed.

"We may get lost or hit a snag," I thought, "but He'll always be there to show us the way to a path He wants us to see and experience." I was just grateful that, after one very hard day and a break from walking as far, Mike was willing to try again, even though I knew his leg was still somewhat sore.

Before leaving The Slaughters Country Inn, we said good-bye to the wonderful waitstaff. Our servers, who referred to themselves as "Tom and Jerry," though one also went by the name "Goober," came over to our table at breakfast to bid us farewell. I took their picture and expressed my thanks to them. We also acknowledged Zoe and Charlotte at the front desk and took their photo before heading out with our driver, Dennis, who took us to Guiting Power, where our walk began.

In the van, we sat and enjoyed last minute views of the inn's vine-covered facades and the forested scenery along the road. The weather was clear but cloudy and cool—in the 50s again. It was 10 o'clock and, though we'd had coffee at breakfast, I still relished another cup. When we drove into Guiting Power, I noticed that the Old Post Office had an A-frame sign in front that announced "coffee." Mike waited for me as I ran in to get a cup.

A village of less than 300 people, Guiting Power was at the heart of a manor owned by King Edward the Confessor, says *Wikipedia*. The name "Guiting" is derived from the Anglo-Saxon word "getinge," meaning rushing, which refers to the Windrush River. The name "Power" comes from the name of the medieval lords of the manor, "Le Pohers."

On the way out of the tiny town, a woman in a bright orange sweatshirt on a white horse with black spots and tail rode unpretentiously by us and waved. We waved back then made our way past several country cottages. Fronted by white-picket and rough-wooden fences, they welcomed locals home to stone-built, vine-covered dwellings with slated roofs, gabled windows, and plaques near the gates that announced names like "Laurel Tree Cottage" or "Castlett House." It's hard to describe the picturesque quality of these places.

Past the hilltop homes, the downhill road grew muddier. We were able to bypass most of the mud, thank God. As we walked past a pile of burning brush, a local man saluted us warmly. The road leveled out after an uphill climb, and we wandered through an open pasture. The miles went by as we tried to follow our arrow on the map. A beautiful area opened up past some tall, flowering pasture-grass, and we could see local estates with large expanses of property in the distance. We turned off a main road to walk uphill beside one estate. The arrow seemed to direct us to the edge of a field at the top, where we turned left and trekked over a very rough trail lined with tall bushes. Then I noticed that the arrow showed us going the wrong way.

"Shoot!" I said out loud. I knew we'd have to backtrack quite a way to get to the right path. Mike was behind me so he wouldn't need to go as far, but, as I passed him on the narrow trail, I told him to wait for me to motion to him. I wanted to make sure I found the right way before I made him retrace his steps. He wasn't happy when I told him we'd been going the wrong way. His leg was bothering him again. But, "It is what it is," I said to myself. I went back to the path beside the estate and watched to see where the arrow pointed. It seemed to indicate a hill straight ahead, continuing into a more obscure area. I went that way, pushing aside brush, and the arrow seemed happy with my choice, so I returned to tell Mike, who waited patiently around the bend. I ended up retracing my steps four times, and I tried to stay positive, despite my impatience with the situation. I explained the mistake

to Mike, and he followed, muttering behind me, toward the correct path. Many trails were almost-hidden and hard to locate. *Ugh!*

The next uphill path was hard for him, but he managed, and we somehow found our way to another trail beside a pasture that led into a forest. I was just thankful the arrow showed us going in the right direction. We passed through a kissing gate and walked through a pretty wooded area full of tall trees and moss-covered logs. The path grew muddy at one point, but we were able to walk around it and rejoin the path where the sludge was less pronounced.

Out of the forest, we crossed a road and were redirected to a scenic path with trees on one side and an open field on the other. We found a nice large stump to sit on, and we rested for a few minutes. We were soon joined by another older couple from Chicago. We chatted for a few minutes, exchanging comments on our walking experiences, where we'd come from and where we were headed, then they moved on. Exiting the wooded area, we crossed a paved road to enter a broad surfaced walkway, where three bikers greeted us. A middle-aged man and his parents, from the area, were out enjoying a ride. We chatted a minute, shared where we were from, then they took off.

As we trekked down the paved walk, a lovely view of rolling pastures with stone walls and green hedges that enclosed farm buildings, crops, and sheep unfolded before us. At the top of a hill, we discovered two large flat rocks on either side of the walkway with a lovely downhill view of a scenic valley. We sat for a few minutes resting and turned to see our Swiss friends coming toward us! We hailed each other again like old friends, and they kept on going. Enjoying some cookies and bars from my backpack, we studied them as they descended, one step at a time, down the hill. It was fun to watch as they became smaller and smaller until they disappeared on the other side of the valley.

On our way, we passed a man rebuilding a wall. One by one, he placed rough-hewn, brick-shaped Cotswold stones on top of each other, fitting each one just right to reconstruct a stone fence. Then we passed by a pasture full of adorable, black-faced, white sheep, who were more interested in us than we were in them. They posed for us in a perfectly assembled quartet. Of course, I had to take their picture.

The walk downhill was easy, especially since it was over a paved path minus the mud. I felt like I was being spoiled. But then we had to take a turn through a gate into a field. At the bottom of the sheep-filled enclosure, we faced the Chicago couple walking toward us across an adjacent pasture. They were lost and couldn't find where the trail continued. I reviewed my map and watched the arrow as it pointed to a hidden gate, which was easy to miss since it was obscured by bushes. After locating it, my arrow showed this as the right way. So, we all walked through the kissing gate and traversed a small bridge into another awaiting pasture.

As we crossed, I walked with the wife as Mike conversed with her husband. The men trailed behind us and, after we'd made our way to the other side of the field, she rejoined her husband. I was only able to find out a little about her. She seemed eager to move ahead. I was coming to find the outlook from most trekkers on this walk to be very different than those I met on the Camino, where everyone was open to talk and share and walk together and find out where you were from and why you were journeying through Spain. The foreigners we'd met here so far seemed reluctant to reveal anything about themselves or ask about you. They seemed more in a hurry to make it to their next destination. It was definitely a different mindset. Maybe it was because this was not a "spiritual journey" per se, and those making this trek were doing it more for sightseeing reasons and not really seeking a deeper meaning or experience. The locals, however, seemed friendly enough.

The pasture led past the impressive Sudeley Castle—the only private castle in England where a queen is buried, says *sudeleycastle.co.uk*. "Queen Katherine Parr, the last and surviving wife of King Henry VIII...lived and died in the castle." King Charles I found refuge here during the English Civil War and "Henry himself, Anne Boleyn, Lady Jane Grey, Queen Elizabeth I, and Richard III have all played a part in Sudeley's story," writes *sudeleycastle.co.uk*. Now, it's used for private venues, like weddings, and it's a tourist attraction. The grounds surrounding the stone-turreted castle are very picturesque. Here, we saw and heard more bleating, black-faced sheep.

Past the castle, we took our time and made our way toward our destination: Winchcombe. On the scenic road into town, two castle guards trotted past us on horseback. Nothing surprised us anymore on this walk! We ascended a road that led to the main street and looked around, trying to decipher which way to turn to get to The Lion Inn, our hotel. Two couples with backpacks huddled together on the corner, and I stopped to ask if they knew where to turn onto North Street. They had just arrived from Holland and were also unfamiliar with Winchcombe. I thanked them and we kept walking.

On this main road—Hailes Street—we passed a wrought-iron fence that fronted a line of picturesque Old English townhomes. The door entries were overarched with porticos decorated with different colored stones. A brick walkway connecting the entryways was lined with pots of pretty plants and flowers. On the other side of the walkway, red and green-leafed trees added more color. Tall stone chimneys towered above the Cotswold-stone dwellings, and lanterns hung over the arched doorways. The year, 1865, was carved in stone above one door. It looked like an inviting little community. I found out this little enclave is called "Dent's Terrace" and was founded by the Dent family of Sudeley Castle in 1865. It's described as "a picturesque terrace of almshouses in multi-colored stones and with gabled porches" by *gilbertscott.org*.

A town of over 5,000, with many buildings dating back to medieval times, Winchcombe is the primary strike site of a famous meteorite that was observed entering the atmosphere in February 2021. The town also once housed a nunnery and a Benedictine Abbey, says *Winchcombe.co.uk.* In harder times during the English Civil War of the mid-1600s, the citizens unlawfully grew tobacco to support themselves. The town's name comes from the Old English words "wincel," a "nook, corner, or sharp bend in a river or road," and "cumb" or "valley."

After passing a honey-stone Anglican church with stained-glass windows above an arched blue double-door and realizing it was the historic St. Peter's Church, we discovered our real destination. An A-frame sign outside a doorway welcomed us into a charming café, and we wandered inside. We were seated immediately at a table for two in a courtyard and served beer and Chardonnay with a satisfying cheese, fruit, and cracker platter. Sitting beside a hand-built stone wall and waving to our Holland friends who sat at a table nearby, we enjoyed every sip and bite.

My determination to "focus on the good things" began to be severely challenged at this inappropriate moment. After giving Mike the "ultimatum" about choices, I was now very tempted to complain because of a spreading "plague" that attacked me. It had all started right after our stay at the London hotel, which made me suspicious. I began to notice some itchy spots on my arm and lower leg. I put cortisone cream on them and hoped they'd clear up. Well, they didn't. In fact, every morning the red bumps spread, first as individual spots and then in groups. So, I couldn't tell if it was an allergic reaction or bed bugs. No matter what ointment I used, or allergy pill I swallowed, they just got worse. The itchy areas had now spread over my lower legs, arms, hands, and even the back of my neck. We wondered if it was a reaction to something I'd contacted on the trail. Maybe the mud exposure on day one of our walk? But why had it spread over areas that were covered by clothing that day and every day since? This didn't make sense. There might have been bedbugs at the hotel, but that seemed unlikely. After trying the cortisone cream, I experimented with other things, like tea tree oil and eczema cream. Nothing. So, on our way to The Lion Inn, we found a pharmacy, and I went inside. I showed the pharmacist my numerous rash-affected areas and asked what might help. He suggested another antihistamine and a different cortisone cream.

After I purchased these, we spotted North Street and crossed over. Not far down the charmingly picturesque row of Cotswold-stone buildings, we saw the hanging wooden blade sign for "The Lion Inn" with a "Welcome" A-frame in front. Inside, we checked in at a bar with Nick, a balding, middle-aged man whose face revealed crinkling blue eyes and lines that cut through his lightly-bearded face when he smiled. He led us through a wooden door and up some winding, narrow, rickety steps to the second floor, right above the restaurant and pub. When he used a skeleton-key to open the door, I felt like I was entering a Dickens-era bedchamber. The modern-looking bed headboards and side tables were out of place next to the old stone fireplace, where an enchanting 1800s-era rocking horse sat ready for a child to hop on and ride. The sloping nature of the floors, the painted chest by the beds, and the small, creaky-floored bathroom added to the charm. We looked around and realized that this was a very old inn that had been revitalized.

Later, we heard someone complain about the inn and how old it was and, admittedly, we could have complained too. The room was small, the floor was unlevel, we could hear sounds from below in the pub and on the street, the shower and bathroom were *very* tiny, the ceilings were low, and it was hard to navigate the steps with our luggage. But, we also contemplated the things we liked about it, and we decided to focus on these. It was clean. The staff was friendly. The beds looked inviting. It was quaint. And it felt like the kind of place one might stay in the Cotswolds, especially 200 years ago! It was definitely different from the other lodging we'd stayed in, but we were only here for one night. Again, it's all about choices!

It was after 4 pm. We'd walked for six hours with some short breaks. Mike laid down to rest, and I decided to look for an ATM machine, since I was getting low on cash, and we might need more if we took a cab or visited local shops that didn't take a credit card. I was directed down to a side street and found one next to a co-op. On my return, I joined Mike for a nap then took a shower. Down for dinner at 6:30 at Nick's suggestion, we were surprised to see that the restaurant and pub were full. "No tables available," said one waiter. We turned to Nick and his assistant, Libby, and they found one for us in a small side room. More helpers! *Yay!*

As I sat, waiting for our food, I was distracted by the itchy, mysterious, and miserable rash, but I wasn't going to focus on that now! I thought about our beautiful walk today and all that we'd experienced along the way. I reminded Mike of what we'd seen. And, when our food arrived, I sat luxuriating, despite the troublesome rash, in this cozy pub in the middle of the Cotswolds as I bit into a heavenly burger and crispy fries and sipped a delicious local beer.

Then, a large, noisy group seated themselves at the table next to ours to celebrate some special occasion, and their laughter and guffaws grew louder with every new round of beer. *Ugh!* Our voices escalated along with theirs as we attempted to converse. But it was no use. Finally, we smiled and looked at each other. Then we laughed. In silent appreciation of the moment, we thought of all the things we were grateful for, like getting here safely, being able to help others make their way, finding a perfect place for lunch, having a comfortable bed to sleep in, and, now, a wonderful and satisfying meal together. We sighed and wondered, again, what surprises the next day would bring us. And, would we be up for them?

Lesson Seven

Be flexible

Beautiful Broadway alleyways

"Flexibility to me means adjusting your schedule to unexpected events, good or bad, and making the most of it."—Cindy Hildner

Early the next day, Saturday, Mike announced that he was very stiff and sore. We'd apparently overdone it the day before, so we needed to take it easy on the way to our next destination, Broadway, which was about 8.8 miles away. We looked at the map—it was about 5.8 miles to Stanton, which was on the way. If we took a taxi to Stanton, the distance from there was still at least three miles to Broadway. Over breakfast, we'd discuss what we wanted to do.

On our way to a table, we noticed two bags by the bar with "Mac's Adventures" tags affixed to them. In the dining area, two ladies sat next to us as we looked over the menu, and I couldn't resist.

"Are you traveling with Mac's Adventures?" I turned around in my chair to address them.

"Yes," they answered. Carol and Joan, in their 50s, were from Canada. "We are on the 'Escape to the Cotswolds' walking tour."

We compared notes, and the only place they were staying which was also on our tour was here at The Lion Inn. It sounded like the distances between towns were about the same on both our tours. We explained that Mike's leg was bothering him, and we might take a break today and grab a cab to Stanton or Broadway. After we explained how he'd twisted it when he grabbed for a branch while trying to maintain balance in the thick mud, they grimaced and shook their heads. Then we all compared experiences with walking in the rain. They'd been caught in it too and had their own explicit, war-weary story to tell. I smiled as I listened to their descriptions of the weather, how it affected their ability to walk, and the places they'd seen. This was the beauty of meeting fellow travelers who'd gone through similar situations and adventures and were willing to share about them. You found out you had so much in common, even at a first meeting. It was what brought you together with complete strangers along the way. And, now, I was thankful to find some who were open to talking about their experiences.

Carol and Joan finished breakfast and were on their way. We took our time. I savored another hearty English breakfast and sipped my juice and coffee. Nick wasn't at the bar this morning, but a woman stepped up and called for a cab. We met our cabby outside around 8:30. Originally from India and Lisbon, he drove us all the way to Broadway. Although I was disappointed that we didn't try to walk at least part of the way that day, in retrospect I think it was for the best that we didn't try. Mike didn't want to complain over breakfast, but I could tell he was suffering from some leg pain. I kept asking him, "What do you think? Should we go partway? Take a cab to Stanton and walk a few miles? Or just have the cab take us all the way?" His answer was always a mumbled response. Nothing definite. But I could interpret the signs. Although I was eager to walk, he was not. His biggest concern was going up and down hills, like the ones we'd encountered between Guiting Power and Winchcombe. These were challenging for him, and trying to tackle more like these would be miserable for us both.

We got into the cab and noticed that the sky was cloudy and threatening rain. Another reason we didn't relish walking without the promise of shelter. We just didn't look forward to another trog through mud. So, hesitatingly, we told our cabby to take us all the way to Broadway. As we drove, we gazed out at the pastures and meadows we were missing. At one point I glimpsed walkers making their way across a field. And I wished I could join them. But I had to focus on the reason for our trip: to experience at least part of a hiking adventure with Mike. And we'd accomplished this over the last three days.

Broadway was a delightful town. As the day progressed, it grew busy with tourists, but it was still scenic, quaint, and worth seeing. And I discovered a few things that helped me to understand the town. The village's name comes from its wide main street, also called High Street, once dominated by great flocks of sheep that brought wealth to the town. Sometimes called the "Jewel of the Cotswolds," it was a prominent stagecoach stop and toll road on the route between Worcester and London in the 18th century. It was also a haven for artists and writers, including William Morris, John Singer Sargent, and J.M. Barrie. The Lygon Arms Hotel, which sits proudly on High Street, once accommodated famous people like Oliver Cromwell and King Charles I.

We arrived before 10 am, when most shops open up, so we walked over blocks of bricked sidewalks, peering into windows, until we saw someone throw open the door to Tisane's Tea Rooms and Garden. We stepped inside and were seated in the front room of this Victorian-style café, and I ordered a mocha. After enjoying this mid-morning delight, I found a store on High Street called Landmark, where I found racks of sporting goods, including jackets, pants, shoes, and trekking gear. Two helpful ladies showed me around, and I was drawn to a sale rack, where I discovered a lightweight, packable rain jacket, shorter than the one I had with me.

We walked behind some street-facing buildings to find a playground where children cavorted as parents and grandparents sat and chatted, and, farther down, a field that led to Broadway Tower. The Cotswolds' highest castle, the tower commands views over 16 counties. *Broadwaytower.co.uk* says: "The Tower is an iconic landmark on top of the beautiful Cotswolds escarpment. It was the brainchild of the great 18th century landscape designer, 'Capability Brown.' His vision was carried out for George

William 6th Earl of Coventry with the help of renowned architect James Wyatt and completed in 1798. The location of the Tower was wisely chosen, a dramatic outlook on a pre-medieval trading route and beacon hill. James Wyatt designed his 'Saxon Tower' as an eccentric amalgamation of architectural components ranging from turrets, battlements and gargoyles to balconies."

We walked across a muddy field, dodging murky ditches, and found a gate that led to a path to the tower. Others were making their way to the site, and we asked how far it was. "About two miles," came our answer. I looked at Mike, who grimaced, and I knew it was more than he could handle. So, we turned around and went back into town. Knowing it was too early to check into the Broadway Hotel, where we were staying, we wandered through an iron gate to use a public restroom on High Street. As I exited the facility, I found Mike waiting for me near the entrance to the Broadway Museum. Just then, a woman, probably the manager, came by and invited us to come inside and check out the museum. So, we did.

We were greeted heartily by a receptionist, who asked where we were from. She talked about how they encountered people from all over the world, and I told her about a refuge on the Camino de Santiago, where a large map on the wall invited pilgrims to place a pin where they were from. I told her that this would be a great way for everyone to see the range of places their visitors traveled from. She loved the idea, and I heard her telling the manager about it later.

The museum was very thoughtfully laid out with rooms full of artifacts, maps, pictures, and a video commemorating the town's long and varied history. I was most fascinated by a large pictorial explanation of "The Cotswold Lion," which told the history of the importance of sheep in the area. "By the late

Middle Ages around 50 per cent of England's economy was due to the profitability of wool," it read. I hadn't realized how much wool had contributed to the country's profitability.

We passed by a large antique table covered with old carvings, large candle holders, and a wooden gameboard set. Under a large, many-paned window, woven wheat valentines dangled from a huge brass ring that sat next to two lidded beer mugs. A tall mannequin dressed in an Old English uniform stood in one corner and a cupboard with glass shelves full of old Broadway pottery sat stolidly in another corner.

After investigating three floors of Cotswold and Broadway history, we felt we had our fill of local lore, and we were ready for a break. Across the street, we found a restaurant that looked inviting but busy with local traffic, which was a good sign. We made our way inside Number 32 and looked at the menu. The food looked right up our alley: a variety of creative sandwiches, salads, and soups. Since we weren't the only ones who thought as much, we stood in a lengthening queue. Fortunately, there were only two of us as compared to large parties of people waiting, so they called our name quickly and seated us.

"Thank God!" I whispered. I was ready to sit down for a few minutes and rest my own legs and feet.

We sat next to a young couple with two small children. We smiled and commented on how adorable they were, and then we glanced at each other with a knowing look. We shared the same "grandparent" thought: "Been there, done that." And, when the kids started acting up, I winked, thinking, "So thankful we're past that now!" We chuckled as we stared at the menu.

"Very creative pizza," I decided as I stared at my "Blanco" pizza with its garlic and rosemary oil base topped with mozzarella, mushrooms, caramelized red onions, and "rocket truffle mascarpone." It was served with mushroom soup, thick brown bread with butter, and sparkling water. I wasn't disappointed. It all tasted even better than it looked.

After lunch, we took another tour down High Street past what looked like a small church now turned art gallery on one side of the street, and a large, historic building that resembled a cathedral called "Old School House" for sale on the other side. I wondered about the story behind this interesting stone building with its row of narrow-paned windows and arched, wooden door entry into a stone portico. It was attached to another building with a bell tower bearing a pointy, "witch's hat" roof with a weathervane on top. A tall chimney behind the tower jutted up from the building, and another row of narrow paned windows decorated the front. Farther down, the same building harbored a tunnel into the lower level of another extension. My imagination rambled about the intent of this old structure and who had once inhabited the numerous rooms. I noticed a clock sticking out from one wall above the arched tunnel. I imagined Scrooge-like men sitting in the rooms with calculators crunching numbers with Bob Cratchity subordinates in the next room shoving wood into stoves to keep warm.

We passed by more cute cafés and shops, one called Sassy & Boo, and then came across some inviting alleyways with rows of stone buildings covered with vines and fronted by hedges as we walked toward our hotel. As in all the other Cotswold towns, many visitors proudly walked their dogs and we had to ooh and aah over a few. The town square held a tall limestone, octagonally-based, cross-topped pillar, much like the one we'd seen in Bourton-on-Water. And it bore the names of locals who died fighting in the two world wars. We walked into the Broadway Hotel at 2 pm, hoping our room was ready.

"Not yet," the receptionist told us. "Come back at 3." So, we made ourselves comfortable in a cozy lounge next to a fireplace with a lit candle inside. Mike settled into a leather chair while I walked around and took pictures of the paintings and decorations in the lobby.

At 3 o'clock, we returned to the front desk and retrieved our waiting luggage. A man helped Mike haul his bag up a few short flights of steps, and I followed. We went around a few bends and past some doors, and I was glad this man was showing us the way. Our room was very nice: twin beds, a chair, a table with coffee service, and a lovely view of a courtyard. I was glad to be able to open the window to breathe in the fresh air, especially since the cloudy morning had turned into a sunny afternoon with no rain in sight. A radiator sat along one wall under the window. The ensuite bathroom was nice, though less spacious than some of the other places we'd stayed. We were just thankful to be in a cheerful, clean, newer, and brightly-decorated place.

We unpacked a few things and decided to rest before going down for dinner. We had reservations for 6:30. At 5:30, we went to the bar for drinks, and we found ourselves among many locals who were making their way to an outdoor patio area. It was Saturday night. Of course it was busy! We sipped our drinks then made our way to Tattersalls, the inhouse restaurant. We met our waitress after being seated at a white-cloth-covered table. In her twenties, Danielle was friendly and welcoming. Her blond-streaked brown hair pulled back into a thick braid, she wore a long-sleeved, blue-gingham top with belted pants. And she had a cheerful demeanor that permeated the ambience and made our experience that night very enjoyable. Originally from South Africa, she came to Broadway for a job, and she seemed to like her new home.

At Danielle's suggestion, we ordered bass with a Chenin Blanc for Mike and chicken with a Chardonnay for me. My chicken was served broasted over mashed potatoes with sauteed spinach and an enviable gravy. As we ate, and appreciated the thought and effort that went into making our dishes, I thought about how our day had not been as challenging as the last three days. I couldn't help but sigh as I thought about the walk I'd missed with the scenic views of black-faced sheep and lush pastures and charming kissing gates and farmers out rebuilding fences and horses cavorting as cows chewed their cud. I regretted not having walked the trails today, but I knew we had to be flexible and not overdo things. And it was nice to take a breather and have time to look around a scenic town. So, I consigned myself to be glad we chose to take this day off from trekking. And I prayed that Mike's leg would be better by the next day.

I realized that, if you are going to travel with another person, or make your way through life with a companion, you have to adjust some preferences to accommodate their needs. This was a challenge for me, but, with God's help, I knew I could do it with a good attitude. I was discovering that being flexible was not just a physical choice. It was mostly a mental one. But that didn't mean I was good at it. I was still learning.

As we sat there, we found out that, sitting right next to us, a young couple from San Francisco were also taking a break from walking through the Cotswolds, and we shared a few similar experiences with them. And, I thought, this was another reason we were here. Oh, how I loved these out-of-the-blue, serendipitous God-encounters!

That night, I prayed, "Lord, help me through tomorrow. And the next day. And the next..." I had no idea what He had in mind for us, but I knew it would end up being good.

Lesson Eight

Get outside of your comfort zone

A graveyard view of the East Banqueting House

"Personal growth is important to me. For me, it's going somewhere new, trying something unknown, meeting strangers, or eating unfamiliar food. All of these things, when completed, help me grow. I find them maybe a little scary, but truly liberating!"—Suzanne Carpenter Taylor

The next morning at breakfast, I caught a glimpse of Danielle with her cheerful smile serving others, and I waved to her. "So nice to see her friendly face," I thought. As we savored scotch pancakes with yoghurt, fruit compote, and Mike's usual—scrambled eggs and smoked salmon, I was drawn to watch a gay couple at a table near us. I'm not sure why. I guess I was fascinated by one of them—a man dressed up with woman's makeup and attire. She looked very glamorous with long reddish hair in a bouffant style, lots of gold jewelry, and a very fancy pants outfit. She was trying so hard to "look the part." And, yet, here I sat, without any makeup, wearing leggings and a wrinkled top that I'd pulled from my suitcase and worn before, with no jewelry except two dots in my ears that were studs you could barely see. I guess, at my age, I wasn't trying to impress anyone. I tried to look presentable, sure, but I was just comfortable with myself these days, after spending so many years trying to look like "somebody." At 71, it didn't matter to me anymore. I had my friends and family, the people I enjoyed at my church, and the neighbors I'd gotten to know over the years.

When I walk my dog every morning and afternoon, I wear very plain, comfortable clothes like leggings, pullovers, maybe a jacket, and my walking shoes. So, I'd gotten used to running into people while I'm out and about. No use dressing up later to impress them when they've seen me that morning in my walking duds or in a robe and slippers getting the mail! That made no sense to me *at all*! They'd already seen my "honest best."

Anyway, I looked over and felt badly that she felt pressured to dress up and act a certain way so people would be convinced of who she was. It made me sad, though I thought she looked very nice for so early in the morning. Later, I saw her in the lobby as I waited for Mike. She descended some steps toward me with a colorful scarf flowing behind her as she bounded down. And, although she never made eye contact with me during breakfast, she did just then. (I guess she couldn't avoid me, since I was standing right in front of her at the foot of the steps!) Anyway, I looked straight at her, and I said, "Hi! How are you?" And she smiled and seemed pleased that I acknowledged her and said, "Good morning!" That made my day, because, besides being a secret agent for God, I want to encourage people and make them feel seen and valued. And I wondered if she had never felt like she was acknowledged for who she was or understood as a person.

As a child, I often felt like certain family members didn't see or understand me. Although I tried desperately to be close to my mom, she made my efforts difficult by often pushing my hopes and dreams aside to emphasize her own desires that I be something or someone other than what or who I was. After growing up with many expressions of disappointment, I wanted others to feel what I hadn't—acceptance. No matter who they were or how they looked. When I read about Jesus's encounters, I see how he did this for so many who were rejected by others, and he changed their lives as a result. My hope was always that I could find that "door" into peoples' hearts where He, along with me, could enter in.

That was the extent of my exposure to her, but I hope my cheerful acknowledgement made her feel a little better about herself. I wanted her to come to know who she was and feel comfortable with that. Wasn't that what God wanted for all of us? To realize who we are and why He'd made us the way we are, so we can thrive in the giftings He's given us, with His help of course. I think so.

I recalled the stories Mike shared about his own childhood. His father, a Navy vet, had started a very successful autobody shop in Omaha, and he was proud of his business. His hope was that his oldest son would follow in his footsteps. But Mike did not share his father's dream. Encouraged by his insightful and determined mom, who saw him for who he was and worked as a server in a school cafeteria to fund his college education, he went on to get a combined Biology and Chemistry degree. He ended up spending years as a lab technician, much to his dad's chagrin. Mike remembers vividly how his father once shoved him across the dining room table during a disagreement, probably the culmination of his dad's frustration with his noncompliant son. I wondered how many sons and daughters are rejected for setting out on their own paths with their own views of how life should be. I think of movies like "Dead Poets Society" and the sadness felt by many kids with oblivious parents. My efforts to be more of an encourager by supporting my children's and grandchildren's giftings, abilities, and aspirations, even when they veer from my own hopes and dreams for them, have grown more expansive over the years. This was one way I was learning to live outside of my comfort zone.

It was still early in the day and too soon to get a cab to our next destination, Chipping Campden. We'd decided to take it easy again to allow time for Mike's leg to heal. Plus, it was drizzling. And I wanted to revisit a shop in Broadway. We talked to Jeannette, the receptionist at the front desk, and she agreed to get us a noon cab. So, I convinced Mike to go with me up the street to the store where I'd gotten my rain jacket. Even though it was Sunday, the stores still opened at 10. We returned to Landmark, and the kind ladies there helped me find some shoes. I'd decided that, since my "water resistant" Hokas weren't all that waterproof, I'd exchange them for a pair that was. And it gave me a reason to get a new pair of shoes. *Ha!* But, sadly, I only had room for one pair besides the pair I was wearing, so I had to leave my older shoes at the store. My new blue waterproof Hokas were brilliant! And they'd keep my feet completely dry if we got caught in the rain again.

Getting new shoes always reminds me of a dream I had years ago where I was standing in a kitchen, drinking coffee, when I turned around and noticed something very odd. As I looked through the door into an attached breezeway, I noticed a row of young people sitting on the floor with their backs against a wall beneath a long screened window. I walked through the door and up some steps, and I approached one of them, a young man.

"Why are you all here?" I queried. He immediately jumped up and pointed to an angled, storm-cellar door on the floor to the other side of the kitchen entrance.

"We want someone to show us how to get through the door!" he answered.

"Oh, I can show you!" I quickly pulled open one of the double doors and stepped down a narrow wooden stairway. The young man followed me. At the bottom of the steps was a spacious arena. On one side, to our left, a large group of people wearing medieval armor, some on horseback and looking like knights, were preparing for a battle. I motioned vigorously to the young man.

"Let's go this way!" I beckoned to the right, and I knew this would lead him to what he was looking for. But the young man was too fascinated by the excitement emanating from the whooping, warlike knights.

"No," he insisted. "I'll go with them."

I was very disappointed that he chose a different route than the one I suggested, but I hoped he would end up in a good place. Sad, and a little dismayed, I ended up at a shoe store, and I bought a new pair. That was the end of the dream. I asked a friend, who was very insightful about dreams, what he thought it meant, wondering if God was telling me to "stop with the shoe obsession," since I had so many shoes already. But my friend had a completely different take on it.

"You need new shoes, because He's taking you in a totally different direction. You'll have a new assignment," he said.

"Wow," I thought. As I considered his words, I looked for how God might be taking me in a new direction. That was over 10 years ago. Now, after 25 years as a financial advisor, I find myself, as a writer, on a completely different path.

After that dream, God gave me another one as a sort of add-on. He took me back to the same kitchen and breezeway, and He showed me that there were still people waiting for someone to come and show them how to get through that door. I've never forgotten those dreams as I've gone about my day-to-day life and travels. And I've kept my eyes open for those young people. I've met many of them along the way, and I'm still seeking more.

Wearing my new shoes, I walked with Mike further up High Street, and we noticed that the town was hosting a dog show in a nearby field. I would've loved watching the local dogs and owners, but we didn't fancy standing in the rain and mud outside. Plus, Mike couldn't stand without discomfort for long periods of time. And, our cab was coming at noon. So, we sadly passed the show signs and walked through an arcade of shops on the way back to the hotel.

We checked in with Jeannette, and I asked to take her picture as she called on the whereabouts of our cab. She agreed but was obviously not used to this request, because she looked demurely down every time I snapped the camera. She reminded me of a female version of Mr. Bean—shy in an engaging sort of way, except with gray, mousy hair. She cracked me up. I did appreciate her willingness to let me take her photo, even though she wouldn't make eye contact. And I was grateful for her making sure our cab was there at noon.

The rain stopped, and the sun came out as we sat at a table in front of the hotel, waiting for our taxi. So much for needing the waterproof shoes. But I still liked how they looked. They even matched my blue pants! The cab turned out to be a van, and our driver took us all the way to Chipping Campden, about 6.6 miles away. I was immediately impressed by this charming town of about 2,500 people as we drove down its High Street.

A market town, Chipping Campden is known for its well-preserved architecture and historical significance. The name comes from the Old English word "ceping," which means market, says *AI Overview,* and the Old Saxon word "campadenu," which means a valley with fields or enclosures of cultivated land. It "received its first borough charter in 1185," according to *Britain Express,* "and a market was established near the present High Street. At that time it was known as Campedene. Within a century the market area was being called 'Cepynge Campedene,' or 'Market Campden.'"

The town's High Street is lined with Cotswold-stone buildings, including Grevel House, built around 1380 by William Grevel, a woolstapler who traded sheep fleeces, says *Britain Express.* The nearby cobblestone-floored Market Hall was built in 1627 by Baptist Hicks, a very wealthy London merchant who gained a knighthood and other honors from James I, because he loaned the king money when he came to the throne in 1603. A former Lord Mayor of London, Hicks also acquired the Manor of Campden in 1612, which was destroyed by Royalist troops in England's Civil War. Market Hall is still used on Sundays to sell cattle hides and sheep skins, and we saw vendors wielding their wares inside the building.

We entered the stone-built, historic-looking Cotswold House Hotel and Spa, where we were staying, and I was impressed by the tall columns beside the front door that supported a portico with letters spelling "Cotswold House" beneath it. The half-circle of fancy, leaded panes above the door made the place look like a 19th century inn. As we walked up the front steps, I noticed an iron fence that surrounded a courtyard, where wicker chairs invited visitors to sit at tables. The location was ideal, since the hotel faced High Street and was across from many shops and restaurants. Not quite as touristy as Broadway, the town felt quainter, and I looked forward to exploring the perimeters. Too early to check in, we left our backpacks by our delivered luggage at the front desk. I asked the receptionist what her favorite place was to eat and, without hesitation, she said, "D'Luigi's across the street." So, we headed that way.

The restaurant was easy to find. Above a sidewalk-row of neatly-placed tables, surrounded by green and white polka-dot-cushioned chairs, hung a sign that said, "Da Luigi Bistro." We headed into the cozy Italian venue and were warmly greeted by a man and a young lady, who seated us immediately. After we ordered lasagna and Montelpulciano D'Abruzzo off the menu, Raffaele, the owner and Luigi's grandson, came over to chat with us. Talking with his hands, Raffaele, dressed in a tight, white, button-down shirt under a blue jacket over even tighter black pants, tossed his light brown, medium-length, styled hair, wild on top, but cut short on the sides, and told us about the history of the restaurant. His grandfather had originally started it in London, he explained, but had somehow ended up moving the restaurant here to Chipping Campden. In his late 30s—rough-shaven and wearing large, horn-rimmed glasses—Raffaele looked the part of a glamour-seeking, big-city, Italian restaurant owner. But that seemed so funny to me, since it was here in this tiny Cotswolds town. I was impressed, nonetheless. I loved his exuberance and joy in serving and welcoming us. He was thrilled to have me take his picture, and he wrote his name down to make sure I spelled it right.

I was even more awed by the fabulous food. The lasagna was some of the best I'd ever had. But, I imagine, when you're served with such charm in an inviting place, the ambiance adds to the quality and taste of the food. And we were definitely delighted.

After this *pranzo speciale*, we made our way down High Street and were captivated by the old stone homes and buildings along the way. I saw one called Fereby House, and I discovered that John Fereby founded the Chipping Campden Grammar School in the early 15th century with his wife Margery. Another fascinating facade, covered with thick ivy that grew over the bow window and front door, fronted Woolstaplers Hall. Built in 1340 and restored in the early 20th century, it served as a merchant exchange. Buyers came from as far as Florence, Italy, to purchase Cotswold wool here, says *Britain Express*. I was interested in a bee-themed plaque on the keystone above the front door, where the doorknocker was a man's face with horns. Apparently, the plaque was hung by Charles Ashbee around 1904 as a pun. The ash wood used, along with the insect, stood for his name, says *offbeatcotswolds.com.* "Ashbee set up many arts and crafts workshops in the village and the tradition of quality craftsmanship continues in the area."

A large home with vines covering the arched windows, and prominent stone balustraded steps with cement dogs at the top, also caught my attention. Spiraling topiaries in large pots sat beside the stairway, and I wondered about its history but could never find anything about it. I still thought it was very charming. Across the street, the renowned Grevel House was the oldest house in town and a good example of 14th century architecture with mullioned windows, gargoyles, and a sundial. On our side of the street, Mike pointed to a square pot next to a stone wall that held a huge, tree-like vine with arm-sized trunks that wound around each other like a braid and were topped by a plethora of greenery.

The oldest inn in Chipping Campden, according to *Britain Express*, is The Eight Bells on Church Street, which dates from the 16th century. Another inn, The Noel Arms on High Street, once hosted Charles II, who rested here after the Battle of Worcester in 1651.

After so many historic finds, we made our way along a flagstone walkway between a thick stone wall and a line of townhomes toward St. James Church. We came to Court Barn and realized it was a museum. We went in and were warmly welcomed by a curator at the door. Realizing how much there was to see, though, and wanting some time at St. James, we decided not to pursue a visit and thanked her. *Shorletspace.co.uk* says, "Later in the twentieth century, Chipping Campden became a focal point for William Morris' Arts and Crafts Movement. C.R. Ashbee, a British designer, relocated his workshop and 50 artisans and their families from London to Chipping Campden's Old Silk Mill. Court Barn Museum honours his work and that of other local writers, designers, and craftspeople." I wish we'd had time to walk through it, but that's how it goes when you only have a day to explore such a unique town.

The lovely old church loomed before us. Within view of St. James's tall square structure, we stood in front of an arched, portico-topped gateway. It was attached to stone walls that swung upward on either side into peaks topped with designs that looked like pointy-topped wheeled carriages. And the walls were connected to two large square buildings with dark-stone "caps." The pad-locked, iron-gated entrance was called the Gatehouse and originally led to Sir Baptist Hicks' Old Campden House. We walked past it to the church. But we were blocked from the entrance by a group of men moving equipment out of the sanctuary into a van. We politely made our way around them to a picturesque graveyard beyond the cathedral. We found out later that a music festival was held at the church the day before. And we were thankful to have avoided that and the attending crowds.

"The parish church of St. James was built in the Norman period, at which time it was known as St. Katherine's," says *Britain Express*. "The prosperity of the Cotswolds during the Middle Ages led to the rebuilding of St. James during the 15th century, under the patronage of William Grevel. Inside the church, a memorial to Grevel calls him, 'the flower of the wool merchants of England.'" Some of the church's hallmarks are a 15th-century brass lectern shaped like a falcon, altar hangings from the 1500s, and a ceremonial cope, a garment worn by a priest, from the 1400s. The church was in existence as early as 1170, when King Henry II visited Campden to confirm the town's first charter.

Inside the entryway, a baptistry with elaborate carvings on seven sides and a brass crown on top sat prominently in the center. The flooring beneath was a unique combination of red, black, and white-patterned tile with a red carpet that led up to the altar past rows of wooden pews. At the front, the ceiling was wood beamed, which seemed unusual for a church. Beside the altar, a black, marble-columned memorial enclosure stood out. "The finely carved canopied tomb of Sir Thomas Smythe is on the North wall in the sanctuary and is the most remarkable in the church," says *happywanderer.com*. "He was Lord of the Manor of Campden until his death in 1593. He lived at the court of Henry VIII and was the first Governor of the East India Company." Near this monument was a black-marble inset dedicated to The Lady Ivliana, the eldest daughter of Sir Baptist Hicks. I found the white marble statues of her and her father inside the inset awe-inspiring.

But, it was the graveyard that impressed us the most. We were completely captivated by the ancient tombstones behind the cathedral. Leaning sideways, covered with algae and lichen, and surrounded by plush, green grass in an enclosed yard, they were the scattered reminders of people who inhabited the area for the last 850 years. The sizes and shapes of the grave markers were fascinating too. Some were cross-shaped, some like clover leaves, and some were diamond-shaped with Celtic designs on the stones, but most were the typical round-topped upright rectangles.

We found a path that took us past the leaning tombstones and noticed tall can-shaped bushes that lined one side of the graveyard. Turning around, I gazed up at the top of the cathedral, which jutted up toward the sky. I noticed that each of the four corners of the perpendicular church was embellished with a pyramid, and many of the narrow pyramids held crosses.

Gazing out from the churchyard, we were mesmerized by spectacular views of pastures on the other side of the stone wall. Off in the distance, we could see a large, picturesque building. We decided to approach it when a passing couple told us we could walk across the adjoining pasture and get as close as we wanted to it. We set out down some steps from the cemetery and turned right down a road until we found a kissing gate behind some bushes that led into the field.

Traipsing between piles of sheep manure and mud through an area called Coneygree, we passed peaceful groups of sheep, who didn't seem to care that we were there, and we walked through the open area as far as we could to catch breath-taking views of the building. After a while, I could tell Mike had gone far enough, and we turned back. But, getting as close as we did to this historic site was worth the effort. Tall, stately, and narrow, it stood out as a landmark across the countryside. Built of Cotswold stone, its honey surface shone under a glowering pink and blue-tinted gray sky. The four corners of its roof held tall pillars topped by cement "flames" that shot into the sky.

Called East Banqueting House, it's what's left of Sir Baptist Hicks' Old Campden House, built in 1610 but destroyed in

1644. Now owned by the Landmark Trust, the house is billed as "an extraordinary Jacobean building whose fine upper room opens onto a terrace overlooking the remains of Old Campden House." For a price, anyone can stay in this three-story building. The couple who explained how to walk toward the house also gave us some interesting trivia. Apparently, after Author Salmon Rushdie wrote *The Satanic Verses* in 1988, he was forced into hiding because some Muslims didn't like how he portrayed Mohammad in the book. For part of his 10-year retreat, East Banqueting House became his safe-haven. That made the house even more fascinating to me. I wondered how someone could stay there for so many years without being found and killed. Apparently, he had around-the-clock police protection.

Making our way back to The Cotswold House, we passed more stately homes and properties—one called Berrington Cottage and another, Coneygree Fold. A picturesque scene opened up past one wooden gate that beckoned up a road to a pretty tree-filled manor. The wooden sign read, "Grace Dieu" or "Grace of God."

"That sums up our trip," I thought as I recalled all the God-winks we'd encountered so far.

We needed that grace when we arrived at the hotel lobby at 2:30 pm, and our room wasn't ready! A different lady sat at the desk—not the friendly one who told us where to have lunch. We saw more bags piled up now beside the desk and large groups of people mingling in the lobby, all waiting to be checked in, and we knew it would be a while. The stressed-out receptionist told us to wait in the bar, attached to the hotel, and someone would come get us when our room was available. So, we went and sat at a table in The Bistro near the hotel's side entrance and waited patiently.

It did feel good to sit down after all the walking we'd done. A waiter came by, and I ordered a drink. As we sat there, twiddling our thumbs, I noticed that the waiter was standing alone at the bar, within feet of us, and that there were no other customers in the place. So, I struck up a conversation with him.

Johann was originally from Sri Lanka, and I asked about his life there and how he ended up here. He shared how he had a good job in London when he was hired by VFS Global, a company that supports governments and diplomatic missions worldwide by helping them with visas, passports, and consular services. But he had to leave his job when his dad in Sri Lanka was dying and needed his help. By the time his father passed away, his savings had dwindled down to 40 pounds, and he had no job to go to. Before his dad died, he told Johann that he knew he would find a wife. Johann wondered how that could happen. Here he was almost penniless and jobless. But, during a real estate transaction for the sale of his father's house, he met a wonderful woman named Kethiki, his real estate agent. They were married three months later! As he told us this story, tears clouded his eyes. His father had believed he would find someone, he explained, and it had happened. His father was a Christian and had showed him the power of prayer. Now, Johann is a Christian. Kethiki is a Buddhist, like his mother, and he prays for her every day.

"She will understand one day," I said. He nodded. Most of his siblings are also Buddhist, he said, so I envisioned him praying for them too.

"Do you go to a church here?" I asked, thinking about supportive people he could pray with.

"I haven't found one where I feel comfortable," he admitted. "But I listen to the Bible every day as I drive here to work."

117

He has a long drive from the town where he lives to Chipping Campden, so he listens to CDs on his way back and forth. Many of the cabbies and hotel staff I'd met lived in areas that were not as touristy, probably because the housing was cheaper.

"I believe in Jesus," he said matter-of-factly.

I shared about my walk on the Camino the year before and how it changed my life and helped me release so many regrets surrounding the death of my own son. I also told him that I hoped we could stay in touch. And I prayed, "Lord, show me if there's more I can say or do for him."

We sat in the bar talking to Johann for at least an hour. Though we were unhappy with the hotel's lack of efficiency with our check-in, we saw how God used this time as an opportunity for good. We'd gotten to know Johann. And he, seeing how long we waited, went to the front desk himself and asked when they could get us into our room. When he returned, he motioned for us to go get our key. They'd check us in now.

But, we faced another obstacle. We had to dig through the pile of suitcases that had accumulated to find ours. Finally, luggage in hand, we dragged our bags up a winding staircase to our room on the second floor, since there was no elevator. Then, our key didn't work well in the door. *Arg!* And we had to fiddle with it for a quite some time until the lock clicked open. Although the room was spacious, it was very rundown and not very clean. I could see dust on all the surfaces, and the "antique" furniture creaked under the weight of our bags. Paint peeled off the walls, and one plastic window blind collapsed and fell on the radiator when I tried to pull the shade down. The bathroom was not very welcoming, especially the not-so-clean narrow tub, old shower curtain, and the door that wouldn't shut all the way. The pipes clanked continuously, and it was difficult to get the faucets to deliver any hot water. It all felt very worn and uncared for. Thank God, we were only there for one night! I was thankful that at least we had a good view of the scenic High Street.

It was the worst hotel on our trip. Nothing was redeeming about it, except for our chance meeting with Johann and dinner that night. Despite the inn's inefficiency and dismal accommodations, the food at the hotel's Fig Restaurant was great. Johann was the head waiter, and he gave us some good suggestions from the menu. We ended up getting a delicious blackened-fish dish served with potatoes and arugula, swimming in a tasty butter sauce. The setting was pleasant, and we were happy that we had this one last chance to see Johann. He was very busy waiting on other tables, but I could tell he appreciated us coming to the restaurant. He made up for the hotel's lacks, and we tipped him generously.

After dinner, it was nice to rest in our room and think about the next day. We were both looking forward to returning to Moreton-in-Marsh and the wonderful White Hart Royal Inn. Mike's leg was still recuperating, so we decided to "cab it" again, and I tried to overlook my spreading rash, which seemed to have a life of its own as it crept up both arms and farther up one leg. The back of my neck looked like I had some sort of contagious disease! But I was bound and determined to enjoy our time here. And I wasn't going to allow this annoying "attack" to be anything more than an irritating inconvenience!

As I gazed at the itchy, clumpy bumps and decided to try yet another salve, this time one Mike had brought along for eczema, my phone dinged, and I got a text message from our neighbor. She sent me a video of our yard, where piles of branches and limbs lay under the trees. Apparently, a severe storm had gone through our area. I thanked her and sent a

119

message to a friend with a tree-trimming service and asked him to swing by our house when he could and pile the debris in the driveway. Later, he texted that he'd done this, and it wasn't so bad, and, by the way, he wasn't going to charge us anything, since another neighbor had offered to pay him for trimming her trees. Yay! Thanks, God! *All good!* I thought. What could have been another disaster turned out to be nothing at all.

"I love how You are in so many things, God!" I wrote in my journal that night. "Now, please heal this ungodly rash!" I thought about how all the potions and pills I'd tried had not really "done the job." Only God could!

And I thought of all the good things that had happened amid the setbacks. Because of Mike's sore leg and having to take a cab here, we had more time to explore Chipping Campden. We'd discovered many charming sites we might never have seen if we'd walked and arrived late in the day. We'd also met some wonderful people: Raffaele and Johann and others.

I wrote: "The benefit of going outside your comfort zone is that you discover more about yourself and how the limitations you imagined can be overcome and surmounted."

This was one of the most important things I'd wanted Mike to experience and me to discover again. And I was looking forward to seeing who and what God would put in our path the next day. Only He knew!

Lesson Nine

Give goodness

One of the gates on the walking paths

"When there are small local stores, I buy my food there to support the local economy. To give friendly words or a smile and interest in people is free. It costs nothing. And you can make friends all over the world."—Nicolette Verkleij

We had one last chance to see what we could in Chipping Campden, now my favorite town in the Cotswolds. I loved how it embraced so many scenic spaces and so much history, along with charming local shops and cafés. Gabor, the hotel manager, checked us out, and, when I asked, he explained how he came here from Hungary. He joked about how his name reminded people of Zsa Zsa Gabor, the actress who was also from Hungary. His engagement with us was encouraging, and, I hoped, it might bring some needed grace to our not-so-amenable stay. But, as we were talking, a very abrupt and stressed girl came out to seat us at a table in the breakfast area, and I sighed. The hotel was in such a great location—convenient to restaurants and historic sites. It was too bad the staff were not particularly friendly or welcoming to visitors. I wondered if it was a "trickle down" situation, where they weren't treated or paid particularly well. We still enjoyed our meal that morning. Mine was my last "hurrah" to an English Breakfast on the trip; Mike continued with his beloved smoked salmon and scrambled eggs. The service wasn't great, but the food was good.

"Lord," I prayed to myself as we ate, "let this day be a great blessing, and help us to meet those You choose. Thanks for wonderful encounters and a chance to do laundry in Moreton-in-Marsh. And an easy train ride to Oxford tomorrow. Thanks!" I had seen a laundromat down the street from The White Hart Royal Inn during our last visit and was looking forward to not only staying at this wonderful hotel, especially after this one, but also being able to wash some clothes!

Since it was Monday, we found some shops closed when we made one last jaunt down High Street. In search of a good cup of strong coffee, we found a bakery open. Small but welcoming, with a prominent list of coffee choices posted on one wall, we drooled over some displayed pastries, but settled on some just plain good coffee. Sipping and savoring a cappuccino, I chatted with a very friendly girl at the counter. It was so refreshing, after the surly staff at the hotel! I asked her how she came to Chipping Campden, and she excitedly explained her journey from Ukraine and her aspirations here. Once again, I was amazed to meet yet another person who had made a sacrificial life change to come here. So far, we'd met people from India, Eastern Europe, South Africa, Kenya, Italy, Sri Lanka, Hungary, and Ukraine. Her cheerful smile and positive demeanor touched me and made my day. I thanked her for doing what she did and for being willing to converse with me.

"What a blessing!" I thought.

I found a pharmacy, which was one objective I had for the day. I wanted to try once more to find something that'd work on my rash. But, it too was closed on Mondays. I *did* find one treasure though—a not-too-touristy shop with attractive clothes and hats, and I purchased a ballcap, now one of my favorites. It says "Messy Weekend" on the front.

"Very apropos," I thought when I saw it. I'd been on the lookout for a cap that said "Cotswolds" or the name of one of the towns we visited, but I could never find one. This would work, though, because it reminded me of how we'd survived a very messy, muddy, rainy trek on our first day here.

We passed another landmark in Chipping Campden: The Bantam Tea Rooms & Guest House. We wanted to go in, but we'd already enjoyed the last sips of our coffee, and it wasn't open yet. We returned to the hotel to sit out front in the little courtyard. We'd ordered a cab for 11:15 am, and we had some time before it came. While we sat in the wrought iron chairs inside the iron fence, I decided to poke my head into the Town Hall next door, where a prominent sign said, "Today! Chipping Campden Art Society Spring Exhibition." I love to peruse the work of local artists, so I left Mike and went to look inside.

Made of the familiar Cotswold stone, the Town Hall has been on High Street since the 13th century. I gazed up at a four-sided clock on the roof at the base of a weathervane-topped belfry. The hall was remodeled in 1897, and it has served the community as a place of commerce, a jail, a school, a fire station, a residential accommodation, a reading room, a town council office, and a community center. Today, it was filled with tables of artist-rendered paintings, photos, and crafts. I walked around, appreciating each artist's wares, and was enthusiastically greeted by two elderly gentlemen who told me about their paintings and encouraged me to buy one. I enjoyed talking to them and hearing their stories. They took my picture, and I took theirs. Mostly I loved their friendly accented banter.

Back at the courtyard, a lady sat near us and talked about a beautiful garden and falconry near Moreton-in-Marsh. I appreciated her input and looked up The Cotswold Falconry Centre on my phone.

"Definitely worth visiting," I thought as our cab pulled up, and we zoomed toward Moreton-in-Marsh. We passed by the centre, and I wanted to stop there, but I knew the amount of walking required to explore it *and* get to our hotel would be prohibitive for Mike.

"Maybe the next time," I thought, wondering if we'd ever come here again.

The eight-and-a-half mile ride was quiet, since our cabby was not very talkative. We jumped out in front of the hotel and made our way into The White Hart Royal Inn. It was 11:30 now, and check-in started at 1 pm. So, figuring it was almost lunch time, we walked up and down the High Street to find a good venue. We tried the Black Bear Inn, but it wasn't serving lunch until noon. Across the street, we spotted Huffkins and walked over. They had a table and were serving, so we sat down amid a bustle of activity. We ordered a garden salad and a chicken salad sandwich with chips. Perfect for us at that moment.

After lunch, we found a pharmacy open, and I got on a list to see the pharmacist. A lady behind the counter took notes on my predicament and told me to wait in line. So, I sat in a chair against the wall next to others until it was my turn. When I was called, I entered a small room and sat in a chair in front of a large desk facing the pharmacist, who was from India. I thought of the friends we'd met at Bella's in London and how the wife told me that many people from her home country pursue careers in the pharmaceutical field.

The pharmacist couldn't tell what had caused the rash, but he prescribed a stronger steroid cream and different antihistamine pills. I was just thankful to have *anything* that might help! Over the next day, the cream worked quickly and helped to clear up the rash. By the time we got on a plane for home, it had subsided significantly. When I told family and friends later about my ailment, some thought it was bedbugs and some suspected the mud I'd fallen into. Everyone had a theory. But a friend who works as a massage therapist confirmed something I suspected, since the rash was only on my lower arms and legs and the back of my neck—areas not exposed during the day but uncovered when I was sleeping. We both surmised that I was allergic to whatever soap the hotels used to wash the sheets. This made sense to me since, at home, I use special allergy-free detergents to avoid breaking out in a rash.

Back to the hotel, we arrived at 12:50 and were shown to our room—up some steps off the lobby. Even though the room was much smaller than the one we'd had the week before, it had a nice view of the street, and it was CLEAN! So much nicer than the one in Chipping Campden. We threw our bags on the twin beds and began tossing dirty clothes into two piles: lights and darks. The same wonderful receptionist named Ana was at the front desk, and, when I went down and asked if she had some plastic bags for our laundry, she went off to the kitchen to find some. So nice! And such a difference between her willingness to help and what we'd experienced at the other hotel. I wondered if the staff at this inn was treated better than those at the other place.

Reflecting on this, I understood that when workers are treated poorly and expected to do more than they can physically accomplish, or underpaid, they get sulky and bitter, and they may take it out on the customers. But I also understood that, even if you're mistreated, you don't have to treat others the same way. And going above and beyond what's expected of you might just open doors to a better opportunity. Reacting to others' negativity by being grouchy and mean is giving "evil for evil" and pays that attitude forward. Giving goodness, on the other hand, even when others don't, can multiply blessings.

I was thinking about a quote by one of my favorite Christian speakers, Joyce Meyer, that I'd read recently in her publication, *Enjoying Everyday Life.* She was talking about how to live the good life, and she said, "Living selfishly is like living in a solitary confinement prison cell."

" *Wow!* " I thought. She also wrote, "Generally speaking, no one means more to us than we mean to ourselves, and when we allow ourselves to live this way, we become lonely and unfulfilled. We are not created to live selfishly, but to reach out to others. As we do, God will give us a life worth living."

" *Yes!* " I thought when I read this. "And being kind and giving goodness, even when we don't receive these from others, are ways we can make a difference in peoples' lives and 'change the atmosphere' around us." I didn't know how Ana was treated by her supervisors, but I was thankful that she chose to be kind and help us at this moment.

We packed the plastic bags as full as we could and ended up with three completely stuffed. Then we set off down High Street toward the side street, where I'd seen the laundromat. We turned too soon but rounded a corner and backtracked up the right street and found it. I had a lot of change and some pound notes and hoped that we had enough for the machines. Once inside, I saw a few machines available in the cramped room, even with several men doing laundry at the same time. I consolidated our loads, so we only needed two machines. The cost was five pence including soap for a wash, so I was able to start them up. But I realized the dryers were 20 pence for only 10 minutes, and I didn't have enough coins to run them more than once, and this wouldn't be enough to get all the clothes dry. So, I had to return to High Street and find a shop that would give me change for my notes. I walked into a hardware store, but the staff there said they had no change. Farther down, a lady pet-shop-owner was very kind and changed my bills. I thanked her profusely and walked back to the laundromat, pence in hand.

Before I'd left to get more change, I'd asked a young man in the laundromat about what coins the machines would take, but he didn't want to be bothered with me. I thought again about Joyce Meyer's quote about living unselfishly. But, when I returned from getting change and realized I was one pence short of having what I needed to dry all the clothes, an older man—a bit disheveled and missing teeth—was kind enough to give me my needed coin.

"You never know, do you?" I thought. "It's like the good Samaritan who stopped to help the man who was robbed. The most unlikely ones are often the people who offer help!" I'd seen it time and time again. It reminded me of what Fred Rogers' mother told him as a child: "Look for the helpers." They will always show up in a crisis!

Then I remembered I had those outdated 10 and 20-pound notes in my purse that no one would take. One store owner told me that a bank would honor them if I had an English bank account. Well, I didn't, and I wasn't planning on opening one just so I could exchange my old notes for new ones. So, I pulled them out of my purse, and I walked over to the man with missing teeth.

When I handed them to him, his lips spread widely across his tooth-gapped mouth, and his eyes lit up and sparkled happily.

"I've been trying to save money!" His face crinkled up under his shaggy hair. "Now, with this, I have a total of 1,000 pounds!" He was ecstatic as he proudly waved the bills.

This made my day!

"How wonderful goodness can be," I thought, "when you find a way to spread it to others."

Hugging our huge bags of clean clothes, we trotted back to the hotel, about three blocks away. I felt like a bag lady going down High Street, as I gripped my overflowing bag. I was outside of my comfort zone, but, at this point, I was just glad to have clean clothes again. I'd worn so many things multiple times over the past week. *Whew!* I looked forward to pulling on some dirt-free pants.

Dinner reservations at The White Hart Inn Restaurant were at 6 pm, so at 5 we went to our favorite corner window-seat in the bar. I got my usual drink and enjoyed feeling clean and dry in my washed shirt and pants. I shuddered when this reminded me of something terrible that had happened on another trip we'd taken just the previous fall.

Every year we plan a car trip with our dogs and enjoy pet-friendly stops along the way. As long as I can remember, I'd wanted to go up in a balloon. Mike and I had even wanted to take off in one after our wedding in a garden. Sadly, the owners didn't allow balloon-rides on their premises. So, Mike gave me a birthday gift the next year of a balloon ride. But, before I could book the flight, the company went out of business. I was so disappointed. That was 28 years ago! Now, our plan was to drive from Kansas City through Colorado Springs, Taos, and Santa Fe, and arrive in Albuquerque, New Mexico, around the time of the annual balloon festival. I'd seen many pictures of the event, and it looked spectacular! I was unable to secure a ride on the day of the festival, so I booked a ride the day before. That was fine, since dogs weren't allowed on the festival grounds anyway, and we'd view the main launch of hundreds of balloons the next day from the surrounding mountains. That ended up being an even better experience! But, since my goal was to not just see the balloons, I was good with securing a flight beforehand.

So, very early the day of my ride, Mike, with the dogs, drove me out to a parking area near the festival grounds, which we'd scouted out the day before. Thankfully we'd seen it in the daylight, because now it was pitch dark. He dropped me off at a gate, and I made my way to where I could see people lining up. They announced where to go based on your ticket number, so I found my post and waited with two friendly couples from Oklahoma, who were also excited about their first balloon ride. While we waited, one of the husbands pointed to the port-o-potties nearby and said he was heading that way. I decided to follow him since I'd been drinking lots of coffee from a thermos and wasn't sure when it might hit me that I needed to go. I knew it would take a while to get the balloon into the air, and we'd be up in the air for at least an hour. So, I followed him in the dark and found one available. I groped my way inside and squatted over the toilet. Suddenly, I felt warmth on my legs and pants, and I realized the lid was down.

"Oh my gosh!" I exclaimed. "I just peed on my pants!" And I had nothing to wipe them with. So, I stood up, pulled up my wet pants, and headed out the door.

I hoped my pants would dry quickly, but they were soaked...in the worst possible areas. Plus, I'd chosen to wear a short jacket, and the wet patches were plainly visible. *Dang!* There was absolutely nothing I could do! I trudged back to the line and faced the two couples, hoping they wouldn't notice the back of my pants or the smell. It was fine for a while, with the wind blowing, but when we headed out to the balloons, I knew people could see the back of my pants, and I was so embarrassed. But I had to proceed to the ride—it was what I'd come here for, and I might never have this chance again. My sole consolation was that I'd never see these people again!

What should have been a wonderful, breathtaking experience, turned out to be challenging and regrettable. Along with 20 other people, I was cram-packed into a huge basket. I stood against the edge and tried to hide my wet pants, but one young couple moved discreetly away from me after a while. I didn't blame them. I'm sure I smelled great! The views were spectacular, and I wasn't at all disappointed by the gorgeous surrounding mountains at sunrise. But I will never forget how disconcerted and discomposed I was the entire time. I was never so glad to get out of that basket and dash toward the waiting car, with Mike and the dogs, after the ride. As I told Mike about what had happened, I wasn't at a point where I could laugh about the horrible ordeal. And, thankfully, he didn't laugh either. I was definitely outside my comfort zone then, but not in a way I would ever want to repeat it! I did learn one thing I'll never forget. Always check to make sure the toilet lid is up, especially if you are peeing in the dark!

Now I sat in my dry, clean pants, and I sighed happily. I also appreciated our meal that night. Dinner at The White Hart was wonderful, with delicious pork pie, mashed potatoes, broccoli, and Rioja wine. We toasted to the completion of our walk through the Cotswolds. Though we'd faced unexpected challenges, we were grateful for the days we did walk through the countryside and the wonderful scenery we saw. We also appreciated having time to savor the amazing food and discover the unique history of each town.

That night, we wondered how it would go the next day, though, when we needed to find our way to Oxford and our hotel, plus figure out how to get around a much larger city.

"We're up for the challenge!" I thought. "After all we've been through, *we can do it!*" I was excited, but a little nervous to explore Oxford, a place I'd heard and read so much about.

Lesson Ten

Never judge by appearances

Students strut through Oxford's streets

"When we don't judge whatever is happening as negative or positive, when we are grateful for whatever shows up, when we see the purpose of any event as beneficial for our growth, when we are grateful for the opportunity to serve, then tumultuous moments are allowed to pass through into purposeful moments or the greatest adventures."—Joy Paguirigan-Kayaban

Today was the day! We'd catch a train to Oxford from Moreton-in-Marsh. This time we'd carry our luggage, since our Cotswold adventure had ended, along with our luggage transfer through Mac's Adventures. Our last breakfast at The White Hart Royal Hotel was a combination of Alpen cereal with yoghurt and fruit for me and Eggs Royale—salmon on a muffin with poached eggs and hollandaise sauce—for Mike. We wondered if the meals ahead in Oxford would be as delicious. After breakfast, we waited in our room for the rain to stop before we headed to the train station on foot. Once at the station's ticket counter, we confirmed when the next train to Oxford would arrive. Then we had to figure out how to get to the other side of the tracks to catch the train. A local helped us by directing us to some steps that led to a spanning bridge. And we stood in front of a small building waiting with a group of people, who confirmed when the right train came screeching to a halt.

English trains are efficient, I found. A recorded announcement lets you know in advance of every stop and reminds you when you are nearing each town. We had plenty of warning for Oxford, which was about 35 minutes away. We sat near the door to get off quickly and found space for our bags on a rack nearby. When it was time, we easily exited with our luggage in tow.

The Oxford station was very busy, more so than Moreton-in-Marsh, because it's a town of 165,200 people, as compared to Moreton's 5,000. "Founded in the 8th century, [Oxford] was granted city status in 1542," says *Wikipedia*. "The city is located at the confluence of the rivers Thames...and Cherwell.... It is 56 miles...north-west of London, 64 miles...south-east of Birmingham and 61 miles...north-east of Bristol. The city is home to the University of Oxford, the oldest university in the English-speaking world; it has buildings in every style of English architecture."

We were able to grab a cab outside the station, and we arrived at the Old Parsonage Hotel and Grill by 11:15 am. The minute we walked up to this historical hotel, we loved it. I was so thankful that this was the place I'd chosen to stay in Oxford. Surrounded by an old stone wall with a gargoyle-topped entrance to its front courtyard, where tables and chairs accommodate visitors, this five-star hotel sits on Banbury Road and has a very unique past.

"The Old Parsonage has stood on the present site since 1660 when Edward Selwood, the prosperous chef of nearby St. John's College, completed the original and principal part of the house...20 years earlier," says *oldparsonagehotel.co.uk*. "Until the mid-14th century, the priest of the medieval hospice, which had reputedly stood on the site since the Norman Conquest, had his dwelling here next to the ancient church of St. Giles, hence the name 'Old Parsonage.' Run by Nuns for the 'poor and infirm,' rent was paid to the church in the form of candles made by the inmates of the hospice.... A bricked-up archway in the present cellar is traditionally associated with a tunnel connecting the house to St. Giles' Church [which still stands near the hotel] as an escape route for priests during periods of religious persecution. The ghost of a nun is said to have been seen in the old part of the house.

"Original features in the present house include the 17th century heavy oak front door...and the wide stone arched fireplace in the entrance hall. The stone window frame in the hall is original.... The front window jambs contain carved gures of saints above sections of guiloch-decorated panelling, all authentic 17th century work in oak."

Today, the Old Parsonage Hotel attracts visitors who enter a cozy beamed lobby with the original wood-burning fireplace. I was particularly attracted to the original 20th century artwork on all the walls. I felt like I was walking through an art gallery. And the welcoming warmth of the staff was also impressive.

We were greeted by a young lady named Nasha at the front desk, who took our luggage and showed us around the hotel premises, including a library, bar, restaurant, and several hallways with rooms. After our guided tour, and a thorough explanation along with a map to demonstrate the layout of Oxford, we sat in the bar and waited to be seated for lunch, which started at noon. The menu looked good, and we ordered a tasty potato and watercress soup and scallops topped with finely sliced radishes and sauce.

After lunch, we got into our room, and our luggage was delivered. Not super spacious, the room was comfortable with attractive decorations, a desk, two comfy chairs, a table, and a view of a garden. We plopped our backpacks on the chairs, gathered what we needed for a trek through town, and set out. Outside, Banbury Road led to St. Giles' Street, where we turned right and passed by St. Giles' Church. On our left, we saw the low-wood-door entrance to St. John's College, one of 43 Oxford colleges. Farther down, we were captivated by The Lamb and Flag pub, and we decided to go back for a brew later.

A passageway beside the tavern led through a high stone-wall-lined space with a huge tree that seemed to grow out of the wall. The passage connects St. Giles' Street with Museum Road and an entrance to Keble College. Farther down St. Giles' Street, we found the stop for a hop-on-and-off sightseeing bus and jumped on one near Broad Street. We found seats in front on top, under a roof and right across the aisle from our guide, Richard, who reminded me of my brother, also named Richard.

He was thorough and entertaining as we drove around Oxford and got a bird's-eye view of the city. We found this a great way to collect information and get a good overview within the hour it took to make the circle back to St. Giles' Street, where we hopped off. The tour was thorough but too quick to take it all in, and I was glad I had signed us up for a walking tour the next day, so we could more closely experience some of these sights, especially the colleges and places I'd always wanted to see.

By the end of the hour, I was desperate for a restroom, and we hightailed it back to The Lamb and Flag. Not even asking for directions, I zoomed through the pub and found the facilities in back. Like so many historic places in England, even the ladies' room was quaint and charming. I joined Mike at a wood-carved table near the front window, and we ordered tall glasses of foamy dark ale. So satisfying!

We discovered that the pub is owned by St. John's College and its profits fund student scholarships. The name of the tavern comes from the symbol of Christ as the Lamb of God carrying a banner with a cross. It's also symbolic of St. John the Baptist and emblematic of St. John's College. The pub was first mentioned in 1772, when it was known as The Coopers Arms.

Back at the hotel, our dinner at the Parsonage Grill was at 5:30, and we sat at a table for two with a cushioned bench along a wall on one side and a chair on the other. After ordering rabbit pie and pork tenderloin, which did not disappoint, we noticed a young Chinese man sitting alone next to us at a table. Wearing a black canvas jacket, with mussed-up hair that hung in clumps over his slanted eyes, he seemed out of place in such a fancy venue. Peering out from his large horn-rimmed glasses, he almost seemed like he was hiding from the world. Mostly he gazed down at his food—a large, thick, juicy-looking steak surrounded by vegetables. And I wondered if he felt welcome in this restaurant, where he sat alone among tables of obviously well-to-do people.

The Lord kept prompting me to speak to him, and it reminded me of another occasion, when the same thing happened.

It was 2011, and we were traveling with a group in Croatia, and my attention was drawn to one couple. At a bus-tour stop in the town of Split, I watched as the husband was escorted to a waiting ambulance while the people on our bus gawked and whispered. And I wondered what had happened to him. Later that week, on the one morning we decided to go to breakfast late, we walked past the couple. I felt a nudge and stopped to ask how they were. They sat with a young man between them and introduced him as their son, Marshall, who lived and worked in nearby Macedonia.

"How did you end up there?" I asked him, being the curious person that I am.

"I was sent by an organization called YWAM," he answered.

"Sure! I know about 'Youth with a Mission!'" He looked up at me, surprised. "There's a church in our area that works with that organization to send young people on missions around the world."

He'd heard of the church, and now I was amazed. He explained that he was sent to Macedonia to help build up the membership of a church and was also working in a local mine, excavating precious stones, to earn money to support himself and the venture. After we'd chatted for a few minutes, the parents, Lyn and Roger, asked if we wanted to join them on an excursion to a nearby island called Lokrum. Since we'd tentatively made plans to visit a beach, I said thanks, but we'd pass. When Mike and I returned to our room to get ready to walk, I felt a strong nudge, and I knew God was telling me that we should join Lyn, Marshall, and Roger on their trip to the island.

"We need to go with them!" I turned to Mike and told him I felt like we should take them up on the invitation. So, we went back to the hotel restaurant to see if they were still there. As we walked into the lobby, we happened to run into them.

"We changed our minds," I said. "We'd like to go with you."

"Great!" they responded, and we walked with them down to the pier where we'd catch a ferry to Lokrum.

The island was enchanting. It was like the Garden of Eden compacted into a small floating space—two miles long and a third of a mile wide. We wandered to the other side, past a botanical garden and an old Benedictine monastery, then we precariously stepped across some large rocks to watch the waves crashing toward the shore. We settled into some nearby chairs under tall leafy trees and enjoyed the view out to the water past the stones.

As we sat there, Marshall began to sing a song that jolted my memory and reminded me of a dream I'd had the night before. In it, I saw a young man singing a similar melody, and, while he sang, something shiny and red caught my eye. I stooped to pick up a beautiful ruby ring that was sitting in the dirt at my feet. I was surrounded by trees, like I was now.

As the scene flashed through my mind, Roger turned to ask his son a question.

"Have you found me a ruby yet?"

He was wondering if Marshall had uncovered any precious stones in the mine where he worked. Again, it reminded me of the mysterious dream. And I wondered what it all meant. As we walked back toward the ferry, we passed a sign with an arrow pointing to where we'd been sitting. It read, "MORE." And I knew God was telling me that there was more to this story. So, I watched to see what He wanted me to know and do. We also saw a spring-fed pool with a waterfall, where people were splashing and having fun. It was called the Little Dead Sea.

On the ferry, we all stood at the back of the boat and watched as we approached Dubrovnik. My jaw dropped when I saw a young man walking toward us on the water! Marshall, standing next to me, was also shocked. Then we realized that the guy was on a waterboard. But neither of us would have been at all surprised if he was skimming the surface like Jesus.

That night, we ate our last meal in Croatia with Roger and Lyn. Marshall had to return to Macedonia, and they invited us to join them. When Roger got up from the table, Lyn whispered that they were separated, because he was a hemophiliac and refused to take needed medication against her advice. On this trip alone, he was bruised and almost bled to death. That was the reason for the ambulance. She was frustrated with his lack of concern for himself, and she'd decided to move away for a while. They were together on this trip so they could connect with their son. When Roger returned to the table, we all decided to leave, and we walked out to the parking lot. There, Mike and I said we wanted to pray with them. Although we knew Marshall was a Christian because of his affiliation with

YWAM, we weren't sure about his parents. But, it didn't matter. We offered prayer anyway.

Huddling in a circle with our arms around their shoulders, Mike and I took turns praying for Lyn and Roger, especially for their marriage. As we lifted our requests up to God, they both cried. We stood for a few silent moments together, then they thanked us, and we said good-bye. We never saw them again.

Back in our room, I told Mike about my dream and what had happened on the island.

"What do you think it all means?" I asked. Then it suddenly occurred to me. "Who can find a virtuous woman?" I recalled the verse from Proverbs 31:10 that speaks of a godly, capable wife. "She is more precious than rubies."

"*Wow!*" I thought. "The ruby Roger is seeking *is his wife!*" I said aloud. "He just hasn't seen it yet. But, hopefully, now he does!" And I knew the young man in the dream was Marshall, whom God wanted to work through, as the missing piece in the puzzle. Through our chance meeting, we were able to put back together the picture of a happy marriage.

Later, I emailed Roger, Lyn, and Marshall about the dream and what God had shown me, and they were amazed. Plus, it just so happened that, on the day Marshall received my email, he was proposing to a young woman on a mountaintop in Macedonia. So, the unusual dream had disclosed many different dimensions of love, healing, forgiveness, and hope for the future. And I will never forget that day and how God used a nudge to open doors beyond my expectation.

Sitting in the Parsonage Grill now, I glanced over at the young man next to us, and I knew what to say.

"Your steak smells so good!" I blurted out, smiling over at him, only a few feet from me, sitting on the same cushion against the wall.

Shyly, he glanced over at me, his eyes barely visible under the bushy bangs.

"It *is* good!" he said. "I got it because I'm celebrating."

There was the door.

"What are you celebrating?" I latched onto the lure.

"I passed all my exams!" he responded.

"Congratulations! What are you studying?" I asked.

"Ancient Asian art," he said.

"That sounds so interesting. Where do you want to work when you graduate?"

"I hope to stay here. There are more opportunities. But I'm not sure how that will work out."

As we talked, I felt God nudge me again.

"Do you believe in God?" I ventured. I usually don't ask this question, because I can tell pretty quickly if a person believes or not. But, in this case, I felt I should broach the subject.

"Yes," he answered quickly. "I am a Christian!"

Shocked by his boldness and willingness to tell me, I said, "That's so great!" then, "How did you come to believe in Christ?"

"I work in a church here," he said. "And my grandmother is a Christian. My parents are Chinese Communists. They are teachers." He looked down.

I thought about his future and understood why he wanted to stay in England. He would be freer here to practice Christianity and pursue the kind of career he wanted. But I could tell he had many questions about what he could do and how.

"Because you have Jesus inside you," I pointed at my own heart. "He can show you what to do and where to go. He can make things clear to you."

He nodded, his dark bangs waving thickly around his eyes.

"What books do you like to read?" I pursued.

"I like C.S. Lewis and St. Augustine. Also G.K. Chesterton," he answered.

I showed him some of the devotionals I was reading on Kindle—books by John Eldredge, David Jeremiah, and Max Lucado. I also showed him how he could message me if he ever wanted to.

"Let me know how you're doing," I said, hoping he would. Before we left, I encouraged him not to be dissuaded from his belief by others. I told him how, when I was in college, a professor told me I was crazy for believing as I did and that I was on the wrong track when I told him I would miss his class because I was attending a Bible retreat.

"I will not let that happen," he said stolidly. And I felt heartened by his stance.

"There are people who will say you're crazy," I reiterated. He nodded. He understood, maybe more than I could know. And I wondered what persecution he'd faced here and, even more so, at home.

When we got up from the table to leave, our Chinese friend also stood up. He wanted us to know he valued and appreciated us. It was his way of showing us honor. I thanked him, and he nodded.

Later, when I thought about how his grandmother had been so influential to him and his beliefs, I cried. This was my hope—that my life would pave the way and clear the brush for my own grandchildren and that, one day, they'd say, "My grandmother showed me this way." Even now, as I think about this, it makes me cry.

I realized how different our evening and the whole day would have ended if I hadn't struck up a conversation with this young man. And I recalled all the nudges. If God hadn't showed me, in so many amazing ways already, that you can't judge by appearances or sum people up by their looks, demeanor, or clothing, or how others react to them, I might not have thought it important to talk to this young man. But, I was learning....

Now, I wondered, as we prepared for another day in Oxford, what the next day would bring. I'd signed us up for a walking tour, and now I asked myself, *Could we manage it?*

Lesson Eleven

Avoid anticipating problems

Into St. John's College's garden

"Expect nothing, or very little. Expectations are the death of things. Look forward to only new vistas, visions, vexations, challenges, and surprises. Great destinations are those where the struggles of travel are adored as much as the destinations themselves."—Baji Surti

We were greeted the next morning in the Parsonage Grill with a wonderful breakfast buffet, but we also ordered kippered herring and smoked salmon with eggs (are you surprised?). The reason for the herring was unique to me. Besides being an English tradition dating back to the 1800s, and one that I wanted to try here, it also brought back many memories.

Ever since I was about nine, I'd savored kippered herring at the Dow Hotel in Freeport, Texas, while celebrating Easter brunch after a church service. Easter was one of the times during the year when my family would venture to my grandparents' ranch for a weekend holiday. It was always three days filled with country romps, climbs up the limbs of huge moss-covered oak trees, and horse rides through fields and past estates around a lake. Every Easter included an elaborate egg hunt around their landscaped property, trying to find the hidden colored eggs we'd decorated with my grandmother. And a traditional Easter brunch with my grandparents at the Dow Hotel. I have no idea how I became interested in kippered herring. I think I ordered it once and liked it so much that I decided this would be my treat every year, and it became my own unique tradition.

While enjoying my English herring, I noticed a 60ish woman, whose styled hair bobbed to her shoulders over a crisp white shirt that was tucked into smart travel pants that fell perfectly to the tops of her energy-efficient walking shoes. She and her husband, who also wore similar streamlined travel attire, were both fit and trim. Suddenly, I had this crazy vision of Sting and his wife Trudie sitting there, dressed up in the latest colorful athleisure wear. My lips curled as I thought to myself, "I definitely don't look like that!" I gazed down at my scruffy, blue and pink fleece pullover with zip-up pockets and my second-day-worn, knee-sagging jeggings. My sorry, dirt-spotted shoes had carried me across parts of Moreton-in-Marsh and Oxford through some rain-sloppy puddled pavements.

"Arg!" I exhaled. "Why am I even thinking about this?" I definitely didn't want to start my day this way! I remembered how I'd compared my attire to the gay woman at breakfast in Broadway, and I did *not* want this to be a trend. I decided right then and there that I wasn't going to judge how others dressed or how I looked. *Not for another second!* Nor would I let myself feel "less than" others who seemed more "put together!"

"Stop it!" I shouted to myself.

It's taken me a while, but I'm learning to be comfortable, no matter how I'm dressed or how others appear, whether better or worse! I guess, when you reach your 70s, you come to the conclusion that life does *not* get easier as you age, so you might as well enjoy every step while you can. And I console myself with my favorite Maya Angelou quote: *"I've learned that people will forget what you said, people will forget what you did, but people will never forget how you made them feel."*

I know that God reminds me many times not to be so concerned with how I look, but to be more attentive to how I make people feel. Sometimes I think that, if you seem too perfect, people may avoid you because you make them feel "less than" what you appear to be. I sighed as I walked out of the restaurant thinking, "But, it would be so nice to wake up and be trim and fit and look like your life is a bed of prim and properly-trimmed roses. *Must be great!"*

On the way to our room, I recalled a celebratory dinner that Mike and I had looked forward to while we were in Stresa, Italy, in 2019. We'd planned a trip to this lovely Lake Maggiore coastal town to commemorate our 24th anniversary and my 67th birthday. Later, we were thankful we'd been able to do this before COVID hit the world scene.

While walking through the scenic and charming town through cobbled alleys filled with lovely shops, we spied a restaurant that seemed perfect for us. Tables were set outside under canopies where guests could sit and enjoy watching passers-by and peer into surrounding shops while tasting wonderful Italian dishes. We made reservations and went back that evening. When we arrived, we were seated at a curbside table for two with a perfect view and handed menus. As we drooled over the descriptions, we were suddenly interrupted by two southern accents.

"Well, what do you know?" said the husband of a couple from North Carolina who were staying at the same hotel as we were. We'd seen them in the lobby, where they'd struck up a conversation with us. We looked up and greeted them courteously and, as we did, our waiter spoke up unexpectedly.

"I can seat you together!" he said enthusiastically.

"Yes. That would be nice!" the wife responded before I could say anything. And, before we knew what was happening, I was being unseated and escorted to a table for four with this couple we hardly knew.

As the conversation progressed, mostly led by the other couple, they proceeded to tell us in a shockingly forthright manner about their multiple face and brow-lifts, including descriptions of the procedures with all the gory details. Teeth gritted, I tried to enjoy the sumptuous spaghetti I'd ordered but soon lost my appetite. Mike and I glanced at each other several times, but we could find no way to exit this cringe-worthy conversation. I tried to change the subject, with no success. When dessert arrived, we ate quickly and excused ourselves. We hurried away with the excuse that we always retire early. Well, that night we *definitely did!* So much for a lovely dinner celebration. I will never forget that night. It made me thankful now that I wasn't *that* concerned about my appearance and how I looked to others! Then, I thought, "Well, it's a new day and I'm glad to be here! *Just as I am!*"

    We set out walking up St. Giles' Street again, back toward the Martyr's Memorial, a huge stone, cross-topped monument at the intersection of St. Giles', Magdalen, and Beaumont streets, not too far past The Lamb and Flag. Built 300 years after the 16th century English Reformation, when the Church of England broke away from the Catholic Church, it commemorates the Bishops of Worcester and London: Hugh Latimer and Nicholas Ridley, who were burned alive on October 16, 1555, after being convicted of heresy because of their Protestant beliefs, says *Wikipedia*. It also honors the former archbishop of Canterbury, Thomas Cranmer, who was executed on March 21, 1556.

    I thought about how I was brought up as an Episcopalian with some of the traditional pomp and circumstance of the Catholics mingled with the less-elaborate Protestant customs. Now, I lean toward a nondenominational church-style, where many non-essential traditions have been replaced with a freer style of worship. But, as I traversed the Camino, I appreciated the meaningful masses in gilded cathedrals and the traditions Catholics have held over many centuries. I especially love their passion. They seem to be able to embrace so many emotions regarding Jesus and what He went through. And this I admire. As a Protestant, I appreciate the freedom of going back to the Bible for a more-original form of worship. I love people I've known on both sides. And so, it disheartens me when I read about hateful conflicts and persecution. I just don't understand it. What I do comprehend is that often it is a purely political endeavor to control groups of people. This makes me sad.

We continued up Magdelan Street and turned left onto Broad Street. We were headed for Ship Street, where we'd meet a student-guided walking-tour group to see some of the famous sites in Oxford. On the way, I stopped at a souvenir shop and got myself a red "Oxford University" ballcap for my growing hat collection. Past more shops and cafés, we spotted the White Horse Tavern, which we'd heard was a famous hangout for the likes of Dylan Thomas, Jack Kerouac, Allen Ginsberg, and Norman Mailer. Then we saw Hertford Bridge, also called the Bridge of Sighs, because it looks like the famous bridge in Venice, and is a skyway connecting the college's Old and New Quadrangles. The Museum of History and Science loomed on one side as we wandered down Catte Street and found the famous Bodleian Library, where the oldest reading room doubled as Hogwarts Library in three Harry Potter films. We walked around the courtyard then the gift shop, since the rooms weren't open yet, and we needed tickets to get in.

Bodleian Library began as a room for a church in 1320 and became a library when Humfrey, Duke of Gloucester and younger brother of King Henry V, gave the University 281 manuscripts, including some classical texts, says *Bodleian.ox.ac.uk*. A new library was built for the books over the Divinity School and opened in 1488. In 1550, the Dean of Christ Church purged the library of all traces of Catholicism, and, in 1556, it was taken over by the Faculty of Medicine. In 1598, the library was rescued by Sir Thomas Bodley, a Fellow of Merton College and diplomat in Queen Elizabeth I's court, and he refurbished it with a collection of about 2,500 books. The library reopened in 1602, and Bodley financed the library's expansion by adding a quadrangle along with a museum and picture gallery. Now it's second in size to the British Library.

Still too early for our tour at 11 am, we walked back to Broad Street and turned left onto Turl Street, wondering if we could find the historical Turf Tavern, which Nasha at the hotel had circled on our map. Not seeing any sign of it, we stopped a local man and asked how to get to it. He pointed this way and that, and we were thoroughly confused, so we decided to walk down Ship Street, which bisects Turl. I found a coffee shop on the little side street, and I stood in line to order a flat white, made with espresso and steamed milk. The local hangout was crowded with young people. As the only senior in sight, I felt out of place. But I was greeted in such a friendly way that I tried to respond as cheerfully as possible to the young people behind the counter. The coffee was terrific. But hot! Sipping it carefully, I wandered back down Ship Street to TSE Noodle, where Mike sat on a doorstep waiting for me. This was our rendezvous spot for the tour, and my eyes gravitated to a young man standing close by.

I walked up to him and asked if he was part of the walking tour. "Yes," he responded. He was from Canada and not the guide. Just waiting, like us. Then, along came a few more, ready to join the tour—a few young couples, an older couple, and some families. Finally, the guide herself walked up—a ballcapped Indian woman in her 40s. We all looked at each other. Not what we expected. We all thought it would be a young student trying to scrape together money for tuition. She was a student, she verified, studying at Oxford and getting a graduate degree. I thought again about not judging by appearances. She turned out to be a great guide—very knowledgeable about Oxford history.

We followed her down Broad Street to the new Weston Library, an extension of the older Bodleian, then to the original library, Harris Manchester College, Radcliffe Camera, Lincoln College, University College, All Souls College, Brasenose College, Exeter College, Jesus College, and Trinity College. Thankfully, she showed us the alleyway to get to Turf Tavern, which was well hidden from the street, and she filled us in on the pub's history. She also revealed an unusual door near Radcliffe Camera with an awning whose supporting arms were decorated with mythological fauns that inspired C.S. Lewis's character in his book *The Lion, the Witch, and the Wardrobe.* We breezed up and down streets and cobbled alleyways, trying to keep pace with her as she engaged us with fascinating facts and entertaining anecdotes.

It was all great, except for one thing—Mike's attitude. At first, I was a little irritated by it. *"Oh, brother! Not this again!"* But, by the end of the tour, I was ready to kill him! And steam was pouring out of my ears! I could tell before the tour started that he was not looking forward to it. His passive-aggressive behavior was a dead give-away! And I wished he'd said something before now. But I'd signed up for the tour months before, I knew we could learn a lot about the town in a short amount of time, and *I* was determined to follow through with it!

"You can sit down and take a break if you need to!" I suggested when I detected some surliness. But my "encouragement" didn't work, and his scowling continued. *Arg!* I felt my blood pressure rising.

Once the whirlwind tour began, at each new site where our guide talked and pointed and explained, he lagged behind, not even trying to hear or catch what she was saying. I knew that he had a hard time hearing, but I didn't find out until later that he had only 10 percent hearing in one ear and 25 percent in the other. Even hearing aids weren't improving his ability to hear very much. When we returned from the trip, he ended up getting a cochlear implant when his doctors realized how poor his hearing really was.

I did know that, though he'd told me his leg was better, he still couldn't stand for great lengths of time due to the past injury and surgeries. I just didn't understand why he wouldn't even try to participate, and I found this irritating. I shuddered, remembering two other times when Mike's lack of hearing terribly impacted our travel plans.

In 2009, we flew to Fiji, thinking this might be one of our favorite trips. It sounded so exotic! I imagined the beaches and palm trees and coral reefs and clear lagoons and tropical fish. What I didn't envision was the intense tropical sun. Nor did Mike, who had not heard the warnings from the staff about how easy it was to get burned.

On our first full day in Fiji, while I attended a company meeting, since this was a business-sponsored trip that required my attendance at a three-hour forum, he saved two lounge chairs near the beach and then promptly fell asleep. By the time I got out of the meeting, he had been laying prone with not enough sunscreen as the shade gave way to penetrating sunrays. On our way to lunch, we quickly realized that his legs and feet were badly burnt. By that evening, he could barely walk as his feet had swollen to twice their size, and he developed silver-dollar-sized blisters on the tops of his feet. We had to cut open his canvas shoes to fit around his oversized protuberances, which now didn't even look like human feet.

After talking to the hotel staff, we got a cab into the nearest town to find a walk-in clinic and pharmacy. Mike had to painfully walk barefoot, like a man with club feet, over bricked pavement, since it was impossible to fit his feet into the shoes now. We found a clinic and a doctor who would see him, but, since he didn't speak English, the doctor handed us a prescription and pointed up the street to a pharmacy. We made our way there and handed the paper slip to the pharmacist, who silently filled the prescription and handed Mike a tub of cream to apply to the raw blisters and second-degree burns on his feet and legs.

That evening, we stayed in our room and ordered room service for a meal that never arrived. So, we ate a can of peanuts.

It was the rainy season, and we grew alarmed as we watched a waterfall develop on one wall by the bathroom and listened to bats fluttering above the ceiling in our room. On one sunny day that week, we sat under an umbrella, making sure Mike, with cream slathered over his feet and legs, had no sun exposure. Above us, a 30-foot palm tree decided to let go of one of its coconuts, and I watched as it fell and bounced off the umbrella above Mike's head. I was thankful to God for the umbrella at that moment. Otherwise, I might have had to tell our family that "Mike was killed by a coconut!"

On another day, we boarded a motor-powered sailing ship that looked like a pirate barque and set sail for some tiny islands around Fiji. Mike waited on the ship while I went for an hour-long snorkeling adventure with others around the island where the movie, *Cast Away*, was filmed. When we returned by dinghy to the ship, tanned and full of tales about the colorful fish that swarmed among the reefs, we found Mike sitting tipsily alone on the boat deck, slugging away his pain with a beer as he waited patiently. I felt so sorry for him.

When our "delightful" week ended, we knew he'd need special care at the airport, since walking was still an issue for him, and his shoes still didn't fit over his swollen feet. We ordered a wheelchair, but, before we could use it, an attendant grabbed the one we had and took it for another person to use. Mike had to stumble awkwardly onto the plane. Thankfully, we were seated in the bulkhead. Other highlights of that unique trip were sitting in the lobby playing cards while rain pounded on the roof and having to wear the same clothes for the first three days, since our luggage didn't make it onto our flight and subsequent flights to the island happened every three days. I had to wear a beach pullup from the hotel gift shop to the company banquet.

On another trip to Amman, Jordan, we were warned by the travel staff, who arranged our trip, not to drink the water at the hotel. Apparently, Mike didn't hear this warning either. *Ugh!*

Assuming the water would be safe in a Marriott hotel, he used the tap water to brush his teeth and take some pills. By the second day, he'd developed a sinister case of "Montezuma's Revenge" and was laid up for two days, staying close to the toilet. The best remedy we found was one suggested by the hotel staff: yoghurt with garlic, parsley, and honey. It did help. Needless to say, Mike missed some of the most interesting tours and points of interest.

When we travel, I like to connect with people and use opportunities that arise to learn from them and speak into their lives. Sometimes I've felt like we were both hindered because of Mike's missed warnings. But, who knows how long he'd been suffering from a lack of hearing! Now, here was another situation. And, not understanding the severity of his condition, I was definitely unsettled. I felt like the tour could be a good opportunity to make at least one or two new friends. We were all here together for the same reason—to learn about Oxford—and it'd be so easy to talk to others and find out more about them and where they'd been and what they recommended seeing.

But *noooo!* I could tell the others in the group were put off by Mike's grumbly, standoffish attitude. Everyone, even the nice older couple, avoided us. And I had to lag behind and wait for him to catch up, because he often would stay as far back from the group as he could—often so far behind that I had to search for him. So, I sometimes couldn't hear what our guide was saying. *Arg again!* I could tell that our tour guide was a bit exasperated with us too, since she had to wait at every stop for Mike to catch up, and he seemed disinterested in what she was saying. When I went to tip her at the end of this hour-and-a-half nonsense, she took my 20-pound note and mumbled a half-hearted reply to my thanks. I was so embarrassed. Everyone else had been joyful and willing participants, even the children of one German couple, where the mother had to translate every word of the guide's message to the kids.

Steaming and ready to explode, I brusquely made my way back to Turf Tavern with Mike trailing behind me. I hoped we could get a table, since it was still around lunch-hour. We found the entrance and a table way in the back. Perfect! I retrieved our table number, glanced at a menu, got Mike's order, and made my way through rooms full of packed tables to the bar, where I ordered. After gathering up two thickly foaming beers and ordering sandwiches, I made my way back to our small table, jammed between others next to a wall. I plopped the beers down on the table and gazed around at this charming tavern. I was so glad we'd decided to come here. My mood lifted a little, but not completely.

Billed online as "an education in intoxication" and "an intriguing warren of small rooms connected by narrow passages and small staircases, surrounded on three sides by delightful patio courtyard beer gardens," Turf Tavern is "located against the medieval remains of Oxford's city walls across…the former moat that surrounded the town, and reached only by exploring the back alleys and cobbled passageways of Oxford's Holywell district." Opened in 1381, it has hosted people like Elizabeth Taylor, Richard Burton, David Bowie, Emma Watson, Margaret Thatcher, Bill Clinton, David Cameron, Boris Johnson, Oscar Wilde, and Ernest Hemingway. The tavern really is a treasure, I decided.

But, as I washed down a cheese toastie (a kind of grilled cheese sandwich) with my beer and watched Mike gulp down his chicken sandwich with a dark ale, I knew I had to get some things off my chest before I exploded. I wanted to share how disappointed I was in how he'd been during the tour and how it made the whole experience quite unenjoyable for me! I understood his leg and hearing issues, but I did NOT understand why he wouldn't even try to participate in the tour.

"What's going on?" I looked up from my toastie and shot him a fiery glance.

"What do you mean?" he responded, and I couldn't believe he could act so innocent and nonchalant, like he didn't have a clue what I was referring to!

"I'm really upset by how horribly negative you've been all morning!" I tried to tamper down my anger and sound like I could be reasonable. But when he didn't respond, I couldn't hold back. "You know, I was *really* looking forward to the tour and seeing as much as we could of Oxford, since we're only here until tomorrow. We may never be back here again! And your terrible attitude and how you acted—like you didn't want to have any part of the tour—really made the experience a bad one for me! It made it so I couldn't enjoy it *at all!*" Ok, I let him have it! Now, *what do you have to say, fella?*

His eyes slowly looked up at me and he got ready to speak. I was ready. I gazed at him intently.

"I get so frustrated," he said slowly, his voice low. "Between my legs hurting when I stand too long and my ears not working, I just feel like giving up."

"I understand all that." My head bobbed up and down. I was really trying to be reasonable. "But, *don't you see?* You gave up even before we started! I could tell you didn't want to be a part of it before the tour began!" I sighed audibly. "I see this sometimes in you and sometimes in other people," I reflected out loud. "They decide even before a thing has happened that they can't do it, because maybe they had some trouble with something similar before. It's gonna be a problem *now* because it was a problem then. I guess I have a different view about things," I paused, my heart slowing down by a beat or two. "I believe if God has opened a door for you to walk through, He'll make a way to go through it. I really think He wanted us to do this today. There were things

He wanted us to see. Maybe about ourselves. There might've even been people we could reach out to or bless." I sighed.

But, as I went on, it all became clear to me in a way I hadn't considered before.

"God can't work with you if you've already decided that He can't help you do it! On the other hand, if you walk into a situation with the attitude that your life is in His hands, and you go in expecting to partner with Him, despite how you feel, then He'll make sure you have what you need so He can work through you." It all made perfect sense to me. And I suddenly remembered the miraculous thing that had happened to me right before I left to walk on the Camino the year before.

I had done as much as I could to prepare to walk on the pilgrimage, but, a week before I was scheduled to fly to France to begin the trek, my hips started acting up, causing me severe pain. Then, my sciatic nerve in one leg began shooting painful nerve-reminders so it was hard for me to sit for very long. *Dang!* I knew I couldn't sit on a plane for over eight hours at one stretch or walk long distances while experiencing this scorching agony. So, I went to a prayer night at my church and, when they asked people to come forward for prayer, I went up to the stage, along with many others, and I lifted my hands up and whispered, "Lord, if you want me to keep standing here, You're going to have to heal my hurting hips and nerve! And, if You want me to sit on a plane for hours and walk miles up and down hills on trails in a foreign land, would You *please* get rid of this pain!"

As I stood there with my hands lifted high, persistently asking, He suddenly released me from the pain. I'll never forget that moment and the miracle I experienced. So, I knew what God could do if you just asked for His help!

I looked again at Mike.

"You can see miraculous healing if you just trust Him, because He wants to work in and through you!" I reminded him of my healing before the pilgrimage. Then I prayed out loud. "Lord, help Mike to see what's possible! Help us both to have the strength and endurance we need to accomplish what's needed! And give me patience, Lord! In Jesus' name. Amen!"

Believe it or not, my little speech and prayer helped us both. Mike's mood completely changed. He apologized for his negativity, decided to expect the best instead of anticipating the worst, and his face changed as he began to smile for the first time that day. I also realized then that there are often things you're unaware of that are going on inside another person, causing them to react in an inappropriate way. His accepting response swept away a thickening cloud that had grown darker over the two of us. Now, we both had more clarity of how to proceed.

"We need to remember to start *every* day with prayer," I thought. We'd forgotten that part this morning. We would've thought of it later, after the day was underway. But, doing it in the beginning would've helped us both be more in sync with each other and with whatever He had in mind for us.

Later I wrote, "One of the biggest lessons we've learned on this trip is to never assume a negative attitude about an undertaking before it's even occurred!" And I felt like it was at Turf Tavern where "the rubber met the road" on this lesson.

We appreciated the rest of the day. On our way to see Christ Church College, we passed by many students in gowns trotting up and down the Oxford streets, swishing their robes as they celebrated having passed their exams, and I was reminded of the Chinese student we met at Parsonage Grill. After entering the college gates, we perused the beautiful grounds, bypassing the buildings, since tickets to get inside were sold out. Scenes from the Harry Potter movies were filmed inside these magnificent, historical structures, and famous people like Lewis Carroll had gone to school here. Apparently, Alice from *Alice in Wonderland* was the daughter of the college's dean, and Carroll first unfolded the story to Alice and her sisters on a boat trip down the River Thames.

We walked past a creek lined with tall grasses, red, pink, and green plants, and a huge willow tree with branches that draped elegantly down to the narrow waterway. The Meadow Building towers majestically on one side of a wide gravel walkway through the campus and welcomes visitors through a gated, arched entrance. Its roof stair-steps up to a point above arched bow windows. From a distance, we could see the famous Tom Tower, named after its bell, Great Tom, and Christ Church Cathedral. But, for now, it was just nice to breathe in the green views around the perimeter and imagine John Locke taking a break in the meadow or walking along the gravel road to class.

After hopping onto another hop-on-and-off bus, we exited near St. John's College on our way back to the hotel. Through an entrance in the stone wall along St. Giles' Street, we approached the college's huge quadrangle surrounded by ancient, honey-stone buildings, some topped with turrets. I felt again like I was traveling back in time.

We walked around the quad and peeked down passageways into adjoining buildings. We were especially lured through an open-gated, archway into a beautiful garden. A gravel walkway, lined with green bushes and trees, escorted us around a large landscaped area. We followed a path that wound around acres of wooded spaces past wooden benches that wrapped around trees, purple flowering trees, multi-colored plants, wood-carved gates, and mysterious doors that led to "secret" passageways. I was enchanted by this unexpected escape—a secluded respite in the middle of Oxford.

Back to the quadrangle, we walked through another archway to exit just as a group of people entered from the grassy enclosure. I heard a woman talking to the group and recognized our ballcap-wearing Indian tour guide from that morning. I called out to her as she passed by, and she looked over and waved. I was surprised when Mike purposely strode over to her. What followed touched me in a way I can't describe.

"I am *so* sorry," Mike held her arm and looked straight into her eyes, "for not being a better participant in your tour. I can't stand very long because I've had two leg surgeries, and I can't hear well. I am *so* sorry."

Our guide waved off his apology.

"That's ok," her face softened.

Then I told her how much we'd enjoyed her tour.

"It made my day!" I exclaimed. And I could tell that we'd made her day, especially since we showered her with praise in front of this new group she was ushering through Oxford. She smiled brightly, and I was relieved that she'd forgiven us for our rudeness that morning. My heart felt lighter and happier at that moment as I sighed and forgave Mike.

We celebrated our last evening in Oxford by venturing down a side street called Little Clarendon, not too far from the hotel, where we discovered a local treat called the Oxford Wine Café. As I chowed down on a wonderful truffle-topped pizza, I watched two parents leaning across the table toward their college student

160

as he dramatically expounded about something outrageous he'd seen or experienced. And I thought about my years listening to my daughter tell her own campus stories about the unbelievable behaviors she'd witnessed from other students. The tales I liked best were the ones she related about her own craziness. Since she was such a serious student throughout her school years, even carrying a briefcase in junior high, these stories amounted to "shocking" descriptions of her spending the entire weekend in her sorority studying for an engineering exam or crying on the bathroom floor because her course expectations were so demanding, while the other girls were out enjoying themselves and partying. And I thought about what an amazing and unusual person she turned out to be. Even today, she takes things very seriously and, of course, her three kids do too, and their lives are stories of applaudable success.

Back at the hotel, one of the waitresses delivered a glass of port I'd ordered to our room. I recognized her from breakfast, and I asked if she'd be around the next day.

"No," she answered. "I'm celebrating my birthday with my husband and kids."

She told me their ages: one month and four years. And I told her to appreciate and enjoy the time with them.

"They grow up so fast!" I exclaimed. When she said she was turning 34, I thought of my son Phil, who passed away at that age from lung cancer. I didn't tell her this. But I did say, "Life is short. Savor it while you can! Because it flies by!"

She nodded.

And I thought about our own ages, 71 and 81, and how fast time had flown by for us and how thankful I was that we could be here and still enjoy each other's company, even after the challenging moments when we let each other down.

"We just need to keep looking at the bright side and be thankful for the excellent moments!" I thought. And it occurred to me why God had put me with this person whose personality was in direct opposition to mine. I was Type A: goal-oriented, risk-taking, and once described as a "Beaver" in a personality test—having a strong desire to do things right, a focus on quality, a preference for structure, attention to detail, dependable, and self-disciplined. Mike, on the other hand, is Type D: stabilizing and cautious, and he could be described as a "Golden Retriever"—intelligent, affectionate, loyal, friendly, and playful. Day to day, though our way of doing things is very different, we are on the same page with our beliefs and what is most important to us. For that I am very thankful.

And, I realize more and more, as time goes by, that we are together for a reason. Though I'm sometimes challenged by his attitudes, as he is by mine, his slower, more deliberate manner teaches me so many things, including patience, how to forgive, and how to love. It's so obvious how God is using two completely different personalities to mold us into better people!

By the way, Mike's cochlear implant has been a real life-changer for us both since this trip. We can watch movies together now, and he doesn't turn to me often and ask, "What did they say?" With his newfound ability, we are hoping for more opportunities to breeze through situations in a more communicative and effective way. He can now engage with others in ways he has not been able to for years. And, we are looking forward to being able to do more in the future. Hopefully minus the lack-of-hearing-caused dramatic disasters!

Now what to do with our short time left here tomorrow? We'd have to catch a train for London in the afternoon. I wasn't looking forward to that, but we'd make the most of the morning while we were here. What unexpected situations would we face this time?

Lesson Twelve

Gravitate to gratitude

Churchill's siren suit

"Attitude and gratitude. Definitely tough times, but there's always something to be thankful for."—Dianne Smyly Brady

At breakfast, I spotted an interesting-looking man sitting across from us in Parsonage Grill. Gray-haired and spectacled, he looked distinguished, and he reminded me of Simon Cowell from Britain's *Got Talent*, especially as he read a newspaper—something rare to see these days! He looked up from gripping his paper as we walked past him.

"I overheard you talking about going to Blenheim Palace," he smiled knowingly. "I highly recommend it! It's not far from here. Very worthwhile!"

"Is it?" I asked. "I've always wanted to see it, and I think we might have just enough time before catching a train to London."

"Yes, yes! You should go!"

I asked why he was in Oxford, and he explained that he met a group of colleagues here every year. They'd gone to school together. He was from the States, and he knew the town well since he'd spent a lot of time here. He asked where we'd been and what we'd seen. We told him about the impressive St. John's College garden and how much we enjoyed walking through the wooded pathway and seeing the flowers.

"Did you go into the chapel?" he asked. No, we had missed that, we said. "They've made it into a venue for entertainment," he said and told us about classical musicians who play there now. "Anyone is welcome," he smiled. And I wondered if they used it for chapel services anymore. I hoped so. We thanked him for his insight and excused ourselves.

At the front desk, we booked a cab to Blenheim Palace for 10 am to return at 2 pm. It was 8:30 now. After packing up our bags, we returned to the desk at 9:30 and left them there to wait for our cab outside. It took no more than 25 minutes to get to Blenheim. The palace is magnificent and a little overwhelming, even from the road. The entrance through acres of tree-covered fields makes the long drive up to the main building awe-inspiring in a reverent sort of way. Originally a deer park, the 2,000-acre estate was first called the Palace of Woodstock. It was a reward to John Churchill, 1st Duke of Marlborough, for his military triumphs, especially the 1704 Battle of Blenheim. Thus, the new name for the palace. The grounds captivate thousands of visitors with multiple landscaped areas and gardens connected by paths that lead past cupolas, statues, and waterfalls. *Wikipedia* says, "Designed in the rare, and short-lived, English Baroque style…. It is unique in its combined use as a family home, mausoleum and national monument. The palace is notable as the birthplace and ancestral home of Sir Winston Churchill."

This was the real reason I was so eager to see the palace. For as long as I can remember, the life of Winston Churchill has fascinated me for as many reasons as there are descriptions of him. I've read at least four books about his life, and I'm always enthralled by the man's ability to "carry on" with obstinate determination, even through continuously torturous opposition. How such an iron-clad and influential man could come out of such a sad and dismal childhood with two completely oblivious parents was also intriguing to me. And how his nanny lovingly influenced his life in such a profound way touched and inspired me. One book I read about him said that, while everyone was moving away from a belief in God toward the science of the day, he requested a copy of the Bible to be sent to him in India, while serving in the calvary, because he remembered his nanny's prayers throughout his childhood and wanted to revisit a faith-filled existence. And, while almost everyone else in the English aristocracy and parliament wanted appeasement with Hitler, especially after experiencing the devastation of WWI, Churchill warned against the dictator's motives, sometimes predicting things in a prophetic way. For over 10 years, he stood alone with his views about what was happening in Germany. When some began to see the signs of Hitler's betrayal of any sort of honest agreement with England, it was Churchill they turned to for guidance on how to deal with the German leader's savagery. And he was the only one who was able to keep a committed and determined-to-win focus during dire days when England was being bombed mercilessly, and America delayed providing much-needed assistance.

A humongous Cotswold-stone gateway with human-sized statues set into the stones on either side ushers you toward the palace buildings, which are giant, columned "arms" extending from one main building to embrace a huge brick-paved quadrangle where people look like ants from a distance. A few decorative cannons sit around the central courtyard. The main building looks like a monstrous columned temple with a triangular roof, where two fierce-looking, winged dragons protect an emblem. A statue of Britannia stands proudly above the entryway and, behind her, two French captives lay chained. Current commentators would have a heyday with this. But I've realized that it's always good to study history to find the reasoning behind things before jumping to too many conclusions. I've tried to apply this logic to my understanding of Winston Churchill's life.

Notable monuments on the property include the Column of Victory, a 135-foot-tall column with a lead statue of the 1st Duke of Marlborough dressed up as a Roman general, statues of Venus around the Upper Water Terraces, sphinx sculptures modeled after the second wife of the 9th Duke of Marlborough guarding the Water Terrace fountains, and a sarcophagus with statues of the Duke and Duchess depicted as Caesar and Caesarina. Pretty heady stuff! I don't think I'd want anyone after my death to think so highly of me that they erected a statue of me as the "Goddess Diana" or "Venus de Milo!" Too much of a legacy to live up to! *Holy hubris!*

The day we visited the palace happened to be a celebration of the "Icons of British Fashion"—a marketing effort to draw crowds, where mannequins stood ostentatiously in several rooms flouting formidable costumes—fashions that represented different stages and ages of British history. Sadly, the icons obscured many famous paintings and some historical fixtures, so it was hard to envision the true nature and quality of the palace interior. Between the mannequins and the growing number of tourists, it became harder and harder to maneuver through the rooms and halls of the mansion. Fortunately, we'd arrived early, so we moved freely through the most important rooms before the crowds came.

I was especially fascinated by a large painting in one room of a looming Churchill, wearing a huge bluish-black robe with a red ribbon on one shoulder and a red cross on another. While his head is capped with a broad-brimmed black hat with pluming white feathers, at his feet sits a cute curly-haired brown dog and a not-so-adorable crowd of WWI soldiers facing him as a young man. To one side of him, a scene of ships is surrounded by flames as a plane zooms overhead. Above, a room full of books entices and a chair sits empty. On the other side stands a row of German soldiers and the Westminster buildings, another flaming ship and plane above these. Over his head, Queen Elizabeth wears a crown next to the Queen Mother with American and British flags prominently beside them. They face a young, school-age Winston wearing a straw boater. And, in front of Churchill, a large letter V made of yellow roses symbolizes victory.

What looks like Vice-Admiral Horatio Nelson's HMS Victory "Battle of Trafalgar" flag unfurls over his right shoulder. Originally a flag officer in the Royal Navy, it was Nelson's leadership, strategy, and unconventional tactics that led to British naval victories during the French Revolutionary and Napoleonic Wars. In life, Churchill looked up to Nelson, whom he considered to be one of the greatest naval commanders in history.

There was certainly a lot to unpack in this one painting! With so many works of art in the palace to capture one's imagination, it was somewhat overwhelming. So, I focused on a few things, like this amazing montage tribute to Winston Churchill in Great Hall. Being a dog lover, I was particularly intrigued by the dog sitting at his feet. Apparently, the pet's name was Rufus—a brown miniature poodle and Churchill's close companion who accompanied him during WWII on his wartime adventures. The dog even sailed with him to meet Franklin Roosevelt. Now I liked Churchill even more!

We saw what we could, walking briskly through each huge, high-ceilinged room, as more and more people entered and pushed us aside to squeeze past, making it hard for me see over their heads, since I am very short. We finally escaped through the front door and found our way to the stables and chapel, where we could wander around in relative peace, with few people to hinder our views. We breathed a sigh of relief.

The chapel held the humongous, embellished pipes of an organ and an impressive marble statue of Queen Victoria holding a scepter and a ball with a cross. But we were more enamored with a special Churchill exhibit in a lower level of the main building, where we found ourselves almost alone. This was my favorite display at the palace. One friendly docent greeted us warmly at the door, and I admired her short hair, mostly because it was what I'd been trying for in a do. I commented on how nice her hair looked and then commiserated to myself on how my own wild hair never behaved as I hoped it would, especially on this trip. It seemed to have a mind of its own, going whichever way it decided to each day. She thanked me and smiled. Later, she helped me by kindly explaining the familial connection between Lady Diana Spencer and Winston Spencer Churchill.

The pictures of a young Winston were enthralling. I loved the ones of him as a baby, a teen in military garb, and a young officer in WWI with his helmet and jacket sitting beside the photo. One case contained his khaki drill dress when he served with the 21st lancers at the Battle of Omdurman in 1898.

"He looked so young!" I thought. I also appreciated the quotes from him on the wall: "Writing a long and substantial book is like having a friend and companion at your side, to whom you can always turn for comfort and amusement" and "Politics is almost as exciting as war, and quite as dangerous. In war you can only be killed once, but in politics many times."

I had read so much about Churchill's "siren suits," which he designed to be quickly donned during air raids in WWII. Two of his one-piece, bright orange and red jumpsuits were displayed in cases. As a Christmas present in 1940, he gave a siren suit to George VI, so the king could be prepared in case he ever needed to enter an air raid shelter. One of the last exhibits was a life-sized mannequin of Churchill standing in front of Blenheim Palace. He was obviously proud of his heritage there. Many of his paintings were also on display, and I remembered that this painting-hobby brought him peace and joy during highly stressful times.

Walking through the grounds, I was impressed by a huge bust of Churchill beside one path. At the end of a paved walkway, a dirt path led through a large meadow down to a waterfall. We needed to head back for lunch, so we took pictures of the scenic view then turned toward the palace. As we went, I decided that our visit to Blenheim was the perfect bookend to our trip to England, with the beginning being a visit to Churchill's War Rooms in London.

I thought we had reservations for The Orangery, a very elegant onsite restaurant near the palace. But, when we got there, they told us they'd sent us an email confirmation with questions, and I'd failed to return the message. So, no reservation. We headed instead to The Pantry, across the courtyard—a cheaper buffet for "the common folk." We found a long line of people waiting to get food and drinks, and we joined the queue. After selecting chicken sandwiches, we found a table in a large, noisy, crowded room. We ate quickly then walked outside, making our way toward our rendezvous spot on a circular drive to meet our cab driver. After waiting several minutes, we got a call from the driver, who explained that he was stuck behind a locked gate nearby. We located him a few yards away, on the other side of a gate, but were told by a guard standing there that we couldn't go through to the other side because of not-so-nearby construction. The guard had been told NOT to let anyone through, and he stood his ground. We found that often the guards and staff, even at nice restaurants, were hell-bent on following the rules, even when they made no sense. I wondered if it was a cultural thing.

So, we slogged a long way, through a muddy field, down and around a fence and then back up to the other side of the gate. It was ridiculous, nonsensical, and very frustrating. A test for our patience, for sure. And our driver was furious.

Wearing mud-caked shoes, we climbed into Amir's pristine, black Mercedes. And he looked on, his eyes wide and

171

staring, at our shoes. I apologized profusely. When we exited the cab, he pulled the mats out to clean off the sticky mud. But now, he knew it wasn't our fault and nodded kindly. On our 25-minute ride to the hotel, Amir agreed to wait for us in the parking lot as we gathered our bags from inside. He would take us to the train station. During our ride with him, we had an interesting conversation. He and his family, who also lived near Oxford, were all from Iran. He, like others from his country, had come here to escape the dictatorial, inflexible regime. I asked him about Iran's involvement with the chaos and fighting in the Middle East, and he squarely blamed the Biden administration for providing funds to Iran's leadership. I thought that was interesting.

We got to the station just as our train pulled up and rode it to Paddington Station. Perfect timing! Then we trekked to our hotel, luggage in tow. Now, the place felt even less charming, since we'd experienced so many lovely and delightful lodgings in the Cotswolds. The one good thing about the hotel was its proximity to the station and the restaurant next door. Of course, we went to Bella's again that night to celebrate the completion of our tour with sumptuous Sangiovese and a lavish serving of lasagna. And, as we sat there, I reminisced about all the wonderful friends we'd met, like Vasenti and Shashti on our first night in London. And the terrific helpers, like Eva and Kirstie at Queen's Head Inn, who saved our mud-covered butts. And all the kindnesses we'd experienced, especially from Kate and Amica in Bourton-on-Water. Of course, we were thankful for the few good things we were able to give, like a few pounds to the man at the laundromat. And the lessons we'd learned, like focusing on the good things and not anticipating the bad. I thought about how Mike had hurt his leg, and we had to take cabs because of it, but how we'd met so many friendly cabbies as a result and had more time to walk around the lovely towns and experience a greater degree of their charming history.

And how God always seemed to work out even the challenging things into something marvelous and good. But mostly, we talked about how important it is to keep an attitude of gratitude, even when things go wrong or not as you'd hoped they would. And we discussed how we'd crossed a muddy field to get to our taxi that afternoon, but we'd found an interesting cab driver who went overboard to help us get from the hotel to the train station on time. And we'd made it back safely to London and were enjoying a fabulous meal!

Even more importantly, we saw again how we *could* work well together, despite our differences, and, oh, how wonderful exploring a different destination can be!

As we sat there reminiscing, Mike grew teary-eyed as he spoke. "I so much appreciated and thoroughly enjoyed the entire adventure, especially the awesome countryside with its history. And meeting the welcoming people. Just being able to walk and experience the trails together...." He stopped to collect himself. "I would absolutely relish doing the whole thing again! And I would enjoy it even more the second time, knowing what would be awaiting us in the Cotswolds."

His expression made me cry, because it encapsulated all I'd hoped to achieve together on this trip.

But then, the conversation took a different turn, and we wondered what life-changing escapades we might experience and what obstacles we could overcome on our next adventure. And we began to make new plans....

A toast to our success at Bella's

Acknowledgements

My heartfelt thanks go to a few people, whose willingness to read my manuscript and give me needed feedback is so very much appreciated. Their comments and input enabled me to finetune the document, especially the details, thus making each escapade and scenario come alive in a greater way. Thank you to Deanne Hurm, Amy Franckowiak, Kay Klement, Charlie and Suzanne Barrett, Connie Smith, Jamie Kidd, Tracy King, Margaret Smith, and my daughter, Charity Steele. Your kind words and helpful suggestions meant so much to me! I also want to acknowledge Brian Skillen and his staff at Publishing Hackers for their incredible assistance and remarkable patience and diligence in helping to make this book come to life! I appreciate all who have touched this story! God bless you!

Read other books by Lele Beutel, sign up for her newsletter, and follow on social media by scanning the QR code or going to the URL below:

linktr.ee/authorlelebeutel

About the author

Lele Beutel and her husband, Mike, enjoy traveling to new places. They have found that, with each excursion, come opportunities to make a difference in people's lives and have their own lives changed as a result. Walking on the Cotswolds was one such adventure for Lele. She considers herself to be a "secret agent" for God because of how He often leads her into unexpected situations where she's able to connect with others. Before retirement, she spent 25 years as a financial advisor and was able to encourage many people mentally, spiritually, and financially through her faith-based advice. Now, she and her husband spend time with their two dogs, Andey and Barney, with grandkids, and as volunteers at their church. They also share experiences with their life group members and the neighbors they meet while walking the dogs.

Other books she has written include:

- *The Camino Connection, Connecting With Life And Commemorating a Death While Walking On The Camino De Santiago,* About Her Healing And Life-Changing Journey Across The Camino;

- *What God Wants You To Know,* a Daily Devotional That Reveals God's Heart Relating To Passages From Genesis Through Revelation;

- *God Answers,* a Daily Devotional With Questions And Answers To And From God;

- *Lele's Selah: Prayerful Poems That Inspire Hope,* And *Flora's Story,* About a Young Girl And Her Family Who Survive The Nazi And Russian Regimes Of 1940s Germany.

To reach her, you can find her on Facebook. Or email her at: *apedersen6@comcast.net.*

She would love to hear from you!